ASSETS FOR LIFE®

PRO[illegible]TY SUCCESS

THE ULTIMATE FORMULA ON HOW TO START, SCALE & GROW YOUR PROPERTY PORTFOLIO TO GAIN FINANCIAL FREEDOM

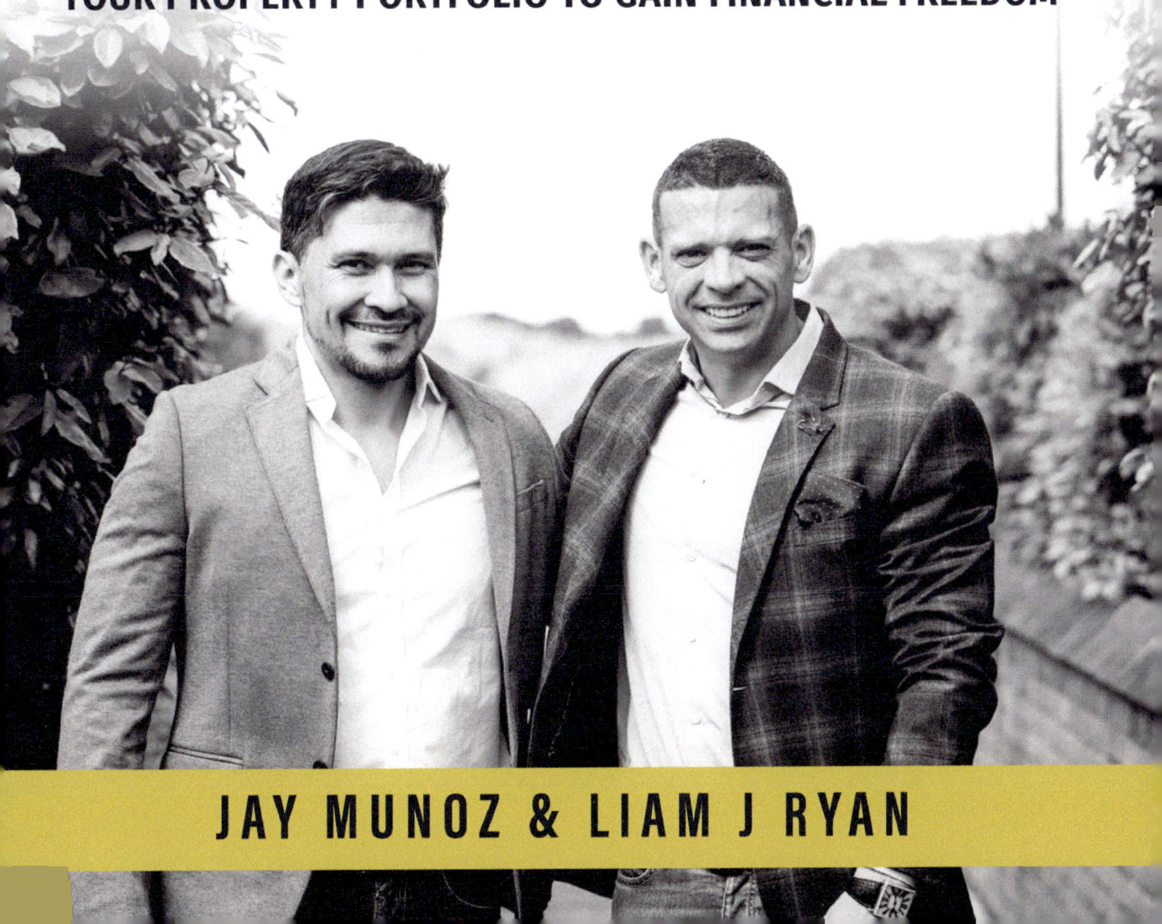

JAY MUNOZ & LIAM J RYAN

ASSETS FOR LIFE®

DISCLAIMER

Author: Jay Munoz & Liam J Ryan

Title: Property Success

ISBN: 9781738417186

Category: Property Investment / Business / Finances

PROPERTY SUCCESS

THE ULTIMATE FORMULA ON HOW TO START, SCALE & GROW YOUR PROPERTY PORTFOLIO TO GAIN FINANCIAL FREEDOM

ASSETS FOR LIFE®

"Education is the foundation upon which success is built. It's the first step in transforming your potential into reality and unlocking the limitless opportunities ahead."

- Liam J Ryan

DEDICATION

Hollie Ryan, my amazing wife - who has always been by my side and supported me in every step of our incredible journey, I couldn't do it without you.

Ida, Charlie, Ivy, and Winter, my incredible kids - you're the spark that lights up my world and the force behind everything I do. You inspire me, every single day, to dream bigger, and push harder.

- Liam J Ryan

To my cherished papà, Luis Gonzalo Munoz Bolanos, whose presence I dearly miss every day. Your unwavering spirit fuels my journey, guiding me until we reunite.

To my incredible half-mango, Ros Munoz, your words of encouragement echoed in my darkest moments, reminding me of my worth.

And to my beloved offspring, Antonia, Carlotta and Luisa, your love and belief in me fuel my determination.

To my dear mama, Diva Mireya de Munoz, alongside my siblings Martin, Lorena and Julieta Munoz, your unwavering support has been my anchor through every storm.

With heartfelt gratitude and kilonewtons of love.

- Jay Munoz

Finally, to everyone in the Assets for Life Family, thank you for being an amazing part of our story no matter how big or small, it means the world to us.

ASSETS FOR LIFE®

PROPERTY SUCCESS

THE ULTIMATE FORMULA ON HOW TO START, SCALE & GROW YOUR PROPERTY PORTFOLIO TO GAIN FINANCIAL FREEDOM

ACKNOWLEDGEMENTS

On behalf of both myself, Liam J. Ryan, and Jay Munoz, we are immensely grateful to everyone who played a pivotal role in the creation of this book.

A heartfelt thanks goes to our incredible team at Assets for Life. Your unwavering support and dedication have not only fueled our business endeavours but have also greatly enriched this project. Your insights and contributions have been invaluable.

We would also like to extend our sincere appreciation to Michelle, whose skillful pen brought our ideas to life in these pages. Michelle, your expertise, patience, and professionalism throughout this journey have been truly remarkable.

Special thanks to Taylor, who diligently worked behind the scenes to gather and organise the necessary information and assets. Taylor, your meticulous attention to detail and relentless effort have been instrumental in bringing this project to fruition.

Together, your collective efforts have helped create a work that we are proud to share with our forever-growing AFL family. Thank you for your hard work, and perseverance, and for being an integral part of this journey.

Liam J. Ryan & Jay Munoz

CONTENTS

INTRODUCTION

OUR STORY BEGINS

> ***"Embrace the journey of starting anew; excellence is never the starting point."***
> ***~ Jay Munoz***

It is great that you have decided to take a step into the property world, and what better way to start or advance than by accessing reliable information from seasoned experts? You might be wondering why we consider ourselves an ideal starting point. With over a decade of combined experience in property investment and a track record of substantial returns, we have navigated the ups and downs of the market firsthand. Let us share our journey with you—how we started, the challenges we faced, and the strategies that led us to success as investors and mentors. What challenges are you hoping to overcome by joining us on this journey?

Hey there, I am Liam J. Ryan!

Here we go then, a little bit about me. My name is Liam J. Ryan and I'm one of the co-founders of Assets for Life, the UK's leading property, business and wealth training company. I created Assets for Life back in 2015 alongside my phenomenal business partner, Jay Munoz. To be frank, I can't talk about myself and not talk about Jay. So, maybe this chapter should really be entitled: Me, Jay and How Assets for Life Began.

"So, how did you and this phenomenal Jay character meet?" I hear you ask. Well, that story began a while back. While you're here, let me take you back to over a decade ago. I was a serial entrepreneur and venture capitalist. I lived abroad for 14 years setting up various businesses and selling them on once they had reached their pinnacle performance. I enjoyed the experience and travelled the world with my various businesses. However, after a significant amount of time away from England, I reached the stage where I simply wanted to be back home. After much deliberation, I decided to move back to the UK and, in true fashion, set up a new business immediately. No sooner had my plane hit the tarmac than I was drawing up plans for a business in the new sector of growth: renewable energy.

Maybe it was my time abroad or maybe it was the research that accompanied my new business venture. Whatever the case, I couldn't help but think about the environment and my kids' future. I wanted to do something that would help to make a positive impact while satisfying my entrepreneurial itch! What's more, the government ran a brilliant incentive to encourage people to buy solar panelling at the time. This meant everyone was a winner. People received a government grant to buy the solar panels and in turn they got free energy for life. A fantastic incentive, but there was something missing. Someone somewhere had to be responsible for selling these panels. "Who would sell these solar panels to the general public?", you ask. Me, of course! It was a win-win situation.

After a great deal of time setting up, doing our due diligence, conducting market research, sourcing office space and carrying out some initial recruitment, the doors finally opened in 2014. We had a gala opening with a ribbon-cutting ceremony attended by all our new staff members. The place was overflowing with champagne and refreshments. It was filled to the brim with balloons, streamers, press coverage, you name it, we had it and then some. It was an unforgettable time, and I felt extremely proud of what I achieved. This was a brand-new company centred around helping our planet and it employed 30 individuals from the local community. What a success!

The business grew rapidly, and before I knew it, we were up to 95 staff members. We took order after order of our lead product, and I was in the throes of relocating our offices to accommodate even further growth. I was living in the fourth dimension. Everything in my life was running like clockwork. I made all the decisions. My stress levels had all but disappeared and because of this, one morning, I decided not to go into the office. That's fourth dimension living for you. I finally had a sense of ownership of my life. Yes, on this day, I was going to do something for myself. On this day, the office could run itself for a while. And so, I decided to go to the gym. My workout had been brilliant. As I stood in the shower afterwards, I was so overcome with joy that I sang, 'Oh What a Beautiful Morning' at the top of my lungs. That's how well things were going, I was singing in the gym shower. The irony was that my song choice was fit for just that - a beautiful morning. The rest of the day turned out to be not so beautiful. Unaware of the bullet about to hit me, I walked into my office, protein shake in hand, feeling pumped up for the day. But the second I walked through the door; I knew something was wrong. There was an eerie tension in the air. It was so real that I could almost feel it against my skin.

All my key staff members looked sheepish, a clear change from the usual warm smiles that welcomed me in. In that moment, no one was willing to look me in the eye. I went up to Donna, my PA, "What's going on?" I asked. for a moment she just stared at me with a slight worry in her eyes.

“Have you seen the latest news?” she asked.

Out of the corner of my eye, I saw staff sneaking furtive glances at us. “I've not seen anything this morning, tell me what's going on.” I replied. Donna ushered me silently into the boardroom and closed the door behind us with a gentle click. I tried to take comfort in sitting on the black leather chairs, but I suddenly became very aware of how empty the room was. My heart beat against my chest as I awaited the news. "for God's sake, Donna, just spit it out, will you!", I barked.

"Liam," she whispered, "the government has just announced that they're cutting the feeding tariff for solar panels. Which means no more government funding for anyone buying their solar panels from us."

Boom. Just like that, the fourth dimension vanished instantly. Everything gone. My business was completely and utterly shattered. It wasn't scalable, it wasn't sustainable, and I knew there and then that over the next few days, I would have to run that business down to its absolute bare bones. It was a gut-wrenching and terrifying shock. Now, I don't know if you can relate to this, but in that moment, it was as though I experienced an eternity all within a split second. My thoughts swam as I realised what this would mean for our employees. I felt terrible for all 95 of my staff members but I had no choice. When it was time to act, I kept the best 10 and said 85 painful goodbyes to all those I had to let go.

Everyone was devastated and I, as a business owner, was practically destroyed. That night and for many nights that followed, I couldn't sleep a wink. Drowning in the anxiety of what was happening, some nights I shed tears over it all. More pain was to follow, a week later, I finally plucked up the courage to go and see my accountants. The final reckoning was yet to come.

My accountants were Dave and John in Billericay, good blokes with bad news. News that I wanted to avoid like the plague, but I had to confront the reality of what was happening. Swallowing my fear, I jumped into my car and drove down to their office. As I arrived, the air was saturated in a distinct musky smell, old coffee. You see, Dave and John absolutely loved drinking coffee. Now, because of the news that came from that visit, the smell of old coffee is a scent that arouses a deep and nostalgic fear in me. I sat down in the chair opposite them, looked them in the eye, and with a frank and nervous sigh I asked, "What's the damage?". David looked at me and gulped hard. He spoke slowly and very quietly.

"I'm very sorry to tell you this Liam," he said, "but you've lost £392,000."

£392,000! Lost! Gone! forever! I stood there; sort of paralysed sort of not, with that musky old coffee smell still sitting in the air. I wanted the ground to swallow me alive. Yet, something chanted on the inside of me saying, "If you don't change, nothing will change, if you don't change, nothing will change." I was gutted, but I had to bite the bullet and get back on the horse. Sitting around focusing on the calamity would solve nothing. It was a horrible week that followed but, I kept my eyes facing forward, kept my team of 10 close to me, and vowed to soldier on. We were still just about able to trade so I turned my attention to trying to generate whatever few sales I could. About a week later, we all sat in silence with most of the life knocked out of us by another gruelling week of minimal sales. Then my office phone rang. One of my admin assistants answered it and a voice on the other end brightly said,

"Hello there, I'm Jay Munoz. Look, I've heard the news and you guys have been calling me for quite some time. I'm now ready to have solar panels installed."

So, my assistant booked the appointment, I jumped into my car, shot down to Colchester and met this Jay Munoz. I was immediately struck by his presence—good-looking, with slicked-back hair and tan skin, he exuded charisma and warmth. There was an instant connection, and I could tell right away that I was in the presence of a genuinely good person. His confidence and down-to-earth nature made it clear we shared similar values and vision. True to his word, he bought some solar panels. As the conversation continued, I asked him what it was he does for work, and he began explaining his work as a property investor to me. The conversation continued, and as he spoke, I realised that we had a great deal in common. His ideas were full of potential. We soon started to formulate a property business model and the rest, as they say, is history.

As well as being a property investor, Jay is also a chartered civil engineer. He's an extremely intelligent guy who gets excited by a spreadsheet. Honestly, his love of numbers is nothing like I've ever seen. I'm the complete opposite! Put me in front of an Excel spreadsheet every day and I'll probably start glitching. So, what do I bring to the table? I am the public face of the company. I get up and do the bulk of any presentations that need doing. I manage the hugely successful Facebook page that yields so very much in the way of connections, awareness and client base. I'm more client-facing. Jay has all the finance and logistics covered off to a T. As individuals, we simply could not have achieved the rapid success of Assets for Life. I'm so grateful to have found a partner who has so many strengths. When I met Jay back in the darker times of 2015, I knew immediately that there was a natural synergy between us where business was concerned. Deep down inside, I felt the faintest glimmer of light at the end of what felt like one of the darkest tunnels I'd ever been in. I had a gut-feeling that we could create something unique and special.

I was immediately struck by the warmth of his personality, his clarity and his business acumen. His credentials were highly impressive too, having worked on some of the biggest builds in the UK as a top project manager for Skanska and ISG. He'd worked on Heron Tower and The Walbrook. He had achieved plenty but there were moments I wondered whether we would be a good fit as partners. After all, it's a big decision to partner with someone, but our partnership was a success and so was our business. The success is found in the million-pound-advice I'm about to give you for free and that is the following:

When choosing a business partner, it is vital you choose someone with opposing strengths and skillsets.

There is no point in both of you being good at the same thing. As mentioned earlier, Jay loves a good spreadsheet! What good would it have been if I loved a spreadsheet too? Or if I also had an engineering degree? Or a background in doing developments?

Individually we both have a broad set of skills, but together, our talents, strengths and abilities combine to create a partnership of extreme versatility and power. This was and is the core of success.
In any business partnership, it's crucial to align on vision, values, and emotional connection. Shared vision and values ensure you support and rely on each other, making tough decisions together. This alignment gives you the best foundation for a successful business.

My encounter with Jay was a gentle reminder that when one door closes, another door opens and that what matters most isn't so much the closed door, but what you do with the opportunity in the form of a new open door. When given a new door, in that moment say, "Yes!". When I knew my solar panel business was over, I had a decision to make. I could continue to wallow and feel sorry for myself or, as an entrepreneur, a go-getter and an action-taker, I could pick myself up and say, "Yes!". Yes, to opportunity, yes to life and yes to trying again. That is how Assets for Life was created.

In nearly a decade, we've added £31 million in property deals and raised over £10 million in joint venture finance. Together, we've built the UK's leading property, business, and wealth training company. We share our knowledge to help you achieve the same success, no matter your starting point. Through the system in this book, you can achieve financial freedom one property deal at a time. I've faced setbacks and made mistakes, but now I'm back, building my empire with the 'No Money Down Blueprint.' Now it's your turn!

You are just 7 steps away from financial freedom. In this book, I'll guide you through each step, with simple actions to implement. Start preparing now for your new future by securing your first joint venture partner and property deal. To succeed, you must take action on each step as outlined. Roll up your sleeves—let's get started. By the end of this book, you'll be ready to take the necessary steps to become a successful investor.

Hi I am Jay Munoz

I was born in Colombia with a privileged upbringing. My parents, both teachers initially, transformed their careers through hard work—my father became a successful homeopathic doctor, and my mother ventured into property development. Growing up in this environment shaped my work ethic and love for building. I had a wonderful childhood with everything I wanted, including a home my father expanded to accommodate the whole family. I attended a top private school, but at 14, something happened that changed my perspective.

"Jay, may I ask you a personal question?". I was puzzled by the request, but I replied,

"Yes." The question was very simple. He asked,
"Are you happy?"

A simple question with a complex answer, an answer so complex that I took several minutes to think about my response. This made me realise that, despite all the material things that I had access to, I was indeed unhappy with my life at the time. This made me step back and reflect on my life journey up until that point. I decided to find the cause of my unhappiness and soon realised that I was being selfish; I was not giving back enough. I concluded that I was then ready to start working on projects to help others, such as volunteering to look after elderly people and working with local orphanages.

After finishing school, I pursued civil engineering to improve lives through better infrastructure. I enrolled at the University of Cauca and earned a BSc (Hons) in civil engineering. The course was demanding, requiring years of intense study and a dissertation. However, the reality is that you eventually specialize, leaving much of the theoretical knowledge behind without ever applying it.

After university, I worked for a construction firm in Colombia, learning modular construction techniques. Wanting to expand my career, I moved to the UK to learn English. I initially chose Eastbourne, but later moved to Brighton due to better job opportunities. I found my first job at McDonald's, which helped me improve my English. While my goal was to pursue an MSc in the US, I decided to stay in the UK. Learning English was challenging, but I persevered by practicing mental narration in English. I also worked hard to save money for a European trip, visiting Spain, Italy, Switzerland, Germany, and France. After returning to Colombia, I decided to move permanently to the UK, where I studied an MSc at the University of Surrey while working various jobs to support myself. I sent out 30,000 CVs, landing five job offers and progressing in my career:

Relax and approach the learning process as a game.

Have a target of learning at least 50 new words a day – both pronunciation and spelling.

The London Underground

The Walbrook and other iconic structures in central London, which cost £150 million to build

EDF new nuclear power station at Hinkley Point C, now worth over £24 billion.

Extension of Puerto Caucedo in the Dominican Republic etc.

Believe that everyone else is happy for you to learn. If you want something from the shop, you need to go there, ask nicely, and they will give it to you.

In 2008, after becoming a Chartered Civil Engineer, I was thriving in the corporate world until I read Rich Dad, Poor Dad by Robert Kiyosaki. This sparked a realization that I needed my own business. It was a 'satori moment' where everything aligned, and I knew I had the knowledge and mindset to change my life. Then I met Liam, an energetic Essex lad, and together we invested £25k for mentorship, using our credit cards. Although it was scary, it was one of the best decisions we ever made, transforming our lives and others'. I'm grateful for Assets for Life.

It ticks all my boxes – I can share and help other people, I can improve lives through building and development both for profit and nonprofit as we have now built three houses for very deprived families who used to live in cardboards in Popayan Colombia (see photos in the legacy chapter), and I have the wealth to have choice and freedom, which means I can give my best to my family too. In the chapters to follow you will learn the tools to start your own property metamorphosis so watch this space.

The Property Freedom formula

Now that you know us—Liam J. Ryan and Jay Munoz—it's time to reveal the core of our success: The Property Freedom formula. This proven system, built from decades of property expertise, is designed to help anyone launch and grow their property ventures. In this book, we explore its mechanics and share client success stories as proof of its power.

The Property Freedom Tech covers everything from building the right mindset and using OPM to choosing sites, appraising projects, and creating a solid exit strategy. This blueprint is your path to financial freedom through property investing. Ready to turn your aspirations into achievements? Let this book be your key to unlocking the potential of the property market.

CHAPTER ONE

MINDSET

> ***Once your mindset changes, everything on the outside will change along with it.***
> ***~ Steve Maraboli***

So, what we are going to talk to you about now and introduce you to in this chapter is very vital in commencing our 7 steps and it is not the first element introduced to you by accident but it is a fundamental tool that we have used to grow our property business. Our graduates have also testified to the difference with which it has enabled them to also build their property business and generate big cash flow. So, let's have a look at step number one which is **MINDSET,** this is the most important step because, if you think you can, or if you think you can't, you're probably right and you have to get into a position where you believe you can go out there and do this, a position where you feel like an unstoppable machine.

So what is mindset?

Mindset is a set of beliefs that shape how you make sense of the world and yourself. It influences how you think, feel, and behave in any given situation. Therefore, an entrepreneurial mindset is a specific set of beliefs, knowledge, and thought processes that drive entrepreneurial behavior. Successful entrepreneurs believe in their ability to succeed and influence their own outcomes, empowering them to take ownership of their lives. The biggest battle you will face, with trying to have and maintain an entrepreneurial mindset is doubt, this inevitably leads to procrastination and then to failure - you will either never get out of the starting blocks, or you quit halfway through.

Maybe you've got a job at the moment working a lot of hours like Jay did for over a decade for several big corporations, possibly right now you've got an employee mentality, what we get to do through this chapter is turn you into having a business owner mindset and an entrepreneur. An employee's life is shaped and governed to some extent by their employer and as such may have a limited mindset - not one to venture into business with. An entrepreneur on the other hand is someone that wants to go and create their own life, someone that wants to build a legacy, someone that wants to make their own decisions - don't get us wrong we are not saying that an employee cannot become an entrepreneur it is just all about the mindset. Creating your own desired life is exactly what you're doing by getting involved with the property business accelerator. In the property world, mindset is crucial because you've got to understand the psychology of landlords, investors, builders, tenants and this list goes on, so really having an understanding that it doesn't matter who you are, or what you do, you can go and do this, is vital to your success. We are so excited for you as further on in this book we will share with you success stories after success stories, and you may realise that some of them actually sound like you - where you are right now.

You see, we believe that one of the main aspects that separates a successful investor developer from the one who struggles is mindset. Having or getting the right information in regards to property investing is important, however, despite having all the knowledge, if you do not have the right mentality, it will all be futile. Now, if you are starting to invest in property for the first time this is not to scare you but more to create awareness of what and how you should think. The property journey gets challenging at times, and believe us, we have learnt expensive lessons from numerous experiences, many issues can come, and without having the right mindset you may end up making some bad decisions that will bring about a great loss or make you give up.

This is where you have to have an outcome-based thinking or be in a solution-thinking state of mind instead of focusing negatively on the issue at hand. It is a continuous battle between a problem and a solution mindset and so having a business mindset encourages a way of thinking that enables you to uncover and see problems as opportunities, your aim is to then have the endurance to turn the situation into a positive - that will make you money but quitting won't. Therefore, you need to have a strong desire, a WHY - The reason that keeps you pushing even when you feel like you want to give up. Napoleon Hill in his book Think and Grow Rich.... stated that "Everything that man creates or acquires, begins in the form of burn desire," always remember that your desire is what is at the root of you taking action.

An entrepreneurial mindset is the cornerstone of sustained success, and perseverance in the face of challenges. It creates an aptitude for pursuing new opportunities, risk-taking, welcoming change, staying focused on what's important and seeing the bigger picture. Understanding the characteristics found in successful entrepreneurs is the first step towards having the ability to become one.

There are five main entrepreneurial characteristics that we believe you should have when venturing into properties:

1 MOTIVATION

Staying motivated is fundamental to success as a property investor, but keeping yourself motivated can at times be difficult. Life does throw curveballs your way and that may interfere with the important investing tasks you have to do. Sustaining motivation is a habit that can be learned. And if you keep at it, it improves with practice. Habits respond to practice just like how the physical body responds to exercise. After going through the myriad advice on this topic, we've boiled it down to a select few. However, one of the key things that we use to sustain our motivation that has taken us to this point of success is constantly asking ourselves this very important question and we would like to ask you that very question now.

Why do you want to become a property investor? If you can't respond to that question explicitly and with enthusiasm, plan to schedule a brief time to figure out or reacquaint yourself with your reasons. Property investing and management is a marathon, not a sprint, and therefore, it's significant to cultivate a long-term view to help sustain motivation. With effective and clearly expressed reasons, you can push yourself to be reminded of the "why" and push yourself to go toward your goals.

2

PASSION

Passion is another characteristic of a successful entrepreneur and not just in the property industry but overall. To be successful as an entrepreneur you have to be able to demonstrate and show evidence of a genuine interest in what you are doing. When entering into the property industry, it's not just your transferable skills and property know-how that will get you to a place of growth and success but a passionate pursuing mindset. The desire to learn more, get mentors, invest in your development, learn from others who are on the path you desire to be and have the heart of love for what you are doing, it has to go deeper than just the love for money. You may be saying if it is not just for money, then what is the point? Well, here's the thing if it is just for money, then what happens when a deal falls through or you hit a loss as opposed to profit? Are you just going to throw in the towel? Passion will help you get back on your feet when you have fallen to the ground. Passion has helped to give us the drive to keep pursuing success in the moments when we were looking failure in the eyes.

3

Vivid VISION

Every successful entrepreneur you encounter or read about likely started with an image or idea related to something he or she felt passionate about creating. This occurs even when the person has no idea how (or if) what they desire to accomplish or create will become a reality. An entrepreneur's vivid vision is the start of a roadmap that will determine where he or she wants to go with their entrepreneurial efforts. A vivid vision is the mental picture of the future you desire. More than just a goal, a vivid vision is the embodiment of our hopes and dreams in a particular area; the picture of what has not yet happened, but what the future may hold. In the property business, having a clear vivid vision is absolutely critical. It is an extremely powerful tool to achieve the results you want, having the mindset and vivid vision to see beyond the dilapidated building standing in front of you. You have got to put your mind, heart and soul into the game. We once read an article that was speaking about vision and saw a quote that really stood out to us from John Graham that we wish to share with you ***"You've got to give yourself the freedom to dream – to use your imagination to see and feel what does not yet exist. A vivid vision is not the same as goals or***

objectives; those come from the head. A vivid vision comes from the heart."

4 CONFIDENCE

There have been times when we have walked into a room or meeting not fully sure how we were going to accomplish what was laying at the forefront of our minds or even deals that have been laid on the table but somehow, we had this confidence in ourselves that we could make it happen. You have read our stories in chapter one and nothing there shows you that we were born this way or always had this mentality. We had to work on ourselves and enter circles of influence that challenged us to grow and build our confidence. Confidence is incredibly important for entrepreneurs to have as it will help you to know that you can achieve your goals, that failure doesn't make you a failure, instead a lesson learnt, this enables others to want to buy what you are selling. Though confidence is necessary, it may not always be easy to achieve. Especially when you feel as if you are constantly being given reasons not to feel confident or successful in your business. People who are not confident can get dragged down by self-doubt and fear and tend to develop imposter syndrome. Entrepreneurs who are very confident are better poised to start and succeed in their business. Because of their self-efficacy, they feel that they are able to succeed. This makes them willing to put in the risk for a new business. Succeeding in that business then builds even more self-confidence. This is because it allows you to feel better -and therefore, be more successful overall.

When you have confidence in yourself you are:

- More likely to go after opportunities
- Better at persistence
- Easier to overcome obstacles
- Others will support & accept your ideas more

5 DECISION MAKING

A question we get asked frequently is how we do so well at decision-making when investing in properties, firstly let us be totally honest here, we don't always get it right. At other times they may ask how we moved from thinking about property investment to taking advantage of profitable property investment opportunities? An important point to make note of here is that fear of investment leads to prevarication and missed opportunities. Whilst jumping in too quickly however could also mean you haven't assessed the opportunity correctly, and your investment is less profitable than it should be. Therefore, patience is as important as not procrastinating. Having a strategy that you work on and get a good understanding of helps. At times we come across clients that want to do everything at once, no! That's not the way to go especially as a beginner, you really want to hone in on what area of property investing you would like to commence with, get the ins and outs so that you can analyse and make solid decisions.

Mindset is absolutely key and should be worked on, on a daily basis. Our option is that there is no 'reality' as such - there is only how we individually interpret reality. Adopting a mindset of success is the best tool you can have to effectively conquer life's biggest obstacles. As Ray Dalio says in his book 'Principles,' to have the best life possible you must first know what the best decisions are, and second, have the courage to make them. We will expand on these two points and say that to accomplish the above, we have to:

- Have clear SMART (Specific, Measurable, Achievable, Realistic, and Time-bound) goals.
- Eliminate the possibility of failure.
- Turn your 'failures' into advantages.
- Find mentors that are ahead of you and learn from them so you get to where you want to be quicker and with less struggles as they have learnt from their mistakes and can help to prevent you from doing the same.

Thrive in discomfort.

Accept conflict as a part of your journey.

Focus on what matters most every single day and avoid the rest.

When talking about mindset and having the right mentality it has to be channeled towards something. A goal or mission that you are aiming to achieve. In the beginning of us coming together we ensured that we had a mission to execute and the why to help fuel us to achieve it. We wasted no time in creating a vivid vision statement for our mission, to help us keep our minds focused or help us get back on track when we got derailed.

When talking about mindset and having the right mentality it has to be channeled towards something. A goal or mission that you are aiming to achieve. In the beginning of us coming together we ensured that we had a mission to execute and the why to help fuel us to achieve it. We wasted no time in creating a vivid vision statement for our mission, to help us keep our minds focused or help us get back on track when we got derailed.

To truly grasp the power of mindset, let's look at the journey of Ashlee Cave, a former secondary school teacher who transformed his life through a significant shift in his mindset. Like many, Ashlee began with a strong desire to break free from the constraints of his demanding job. Despite working over 70 hours a week, he yearned for more control over his time and financial future. However, it wasn't until Ashlee decided to fully embrace an entrepreneurial mindset that his life began to change. By applying the principles discussed in this chapter, he pushed past his initial fears and doubts, overcoming the challenges of the COVID crisis and securing his first investor through persistence and consistent effort. Today, Ashlee runs a successful six-figure property business, has reduced his teaching role to a part-time commitment by choice, and is now mentoring others. His story is a testament to the transformative power of a strong, entrepreneurial mindset. When you believe in your potential and take decisive action, like Ashlee did, you can achieve extraordinary results. You can find out more about Ashlee's inspiring journey in the final chapter of this book.

MISSION

So, if you have a vision statement or have been thinking about it then great, if not, you will need to take some time to create one for yourself or your business.

So, what is a mission?

A mission combines what you do with what the world needs. In business and property, focusing on strategies that fulfill real-world demands is crucial. Land is finite, housing demand exceeds supply, and property prices and rents have been steadily rising, doubling every decade since 1088. Property is essential, making it a valuable sector to work in.

Your mission should align with your skills, passions, the world's needs, and profitability. Many entrepreneurs struggle because they fail to address market demand. As a business owner, you must be self-sufficient, motivated, and take full responsibility for decisions—you're the leader of your ship. Property is not just a want but a necessity, offering significant opportunities for impact and income while fulfilling a critical need.

An entrepreneurial mindset transforms how you approach opportunities and challenges in the property market. It drives action, persistence, and success, turning obstacles into opportunities. With the principles in this chapter, you can build a mindset that envisions and achieves success. Nurture it wisely, and watch your property investing dreams become reality.

Assignment

Mindset Reflection and Action Plan

1. **Reflection:** Take a moment to reflect on your current mindset towards property investing. Write down your thoughts about the following questions:

- What aspects of my current mindset might be limiting my success in property investments?
- Which traits of a successful entrepreneurial mindset do I already possess, and which do I need to develop further?

2

Vision Board: Create a vision board that represents your goals and aspirations as a property investor. Include images, quotes, and symbols that resonate with your ambitions and the mindset you aim to cultivate. This visual representation will serve as a daily reminder of where you're headed and the mindset you need to uphold.

3

Action Plan: Based on your reflections and the characteristics of a successful entrepreneurial mindset discussed in this chapter, draft a concrete action plan. Outline specific steps you will take over the next month to strengthen your entrepreneurial mindset. This could include:

- Reading books or listening to podcasts that inspire and build entrepreneurial skills.
- Attending a workshop or seminar on property investing.
- Networking with other investors to learn and grow.
- Setting daily affirmations that reinforce your commitment and confidence.

4

Journal: Commit to a daily or weekly journaling practice focused on your mindset journey. After each property-related activity or decision, jot down what went well, what challenges you encountered, and how you can improve. Reflect on how your mindset influenced the outcomes and what shifts you might need to make. for this you can use My AFL journey created specifically for you by Jay Munoz. You can grab a copy from amazon for only £5!

This assignment is designed to make the abstract concept of mindset tangible and actionable. By completing these tasks, you will not only reinforce the lessons learned in this chapter but also begin to see real changes in how you approach your investments. Remember, the journey to becoming a successful property investor is both challenging and rewarding—your mindset is your most powerful tool on this journey.

EMPOWERED AND READY TO BEGIN? EXPLORE OUR EVENTS AND GET STARTED TODAY!

ASSETS FOR LIFE®

CHAPTER TWO

FUNDING

This is our favorite step of all the property freedom formula steps. In this chapter, we will teach you the various types of funding you can venture into when on your property business journey. We will look at getting investors, different types of products your investors can be investing in, mortgages, the different types of development funding and bridging finance. It's going to be a very, very exciting chapter. Funding is step two of the property freedom formula and at this point we would like to ask you, what do you believe comes first, do you get the money first, and then the deal or do you get the deal first, and then get the money? We believe they pretty much work hand in hand.

Ultimately, where you want to get to is being in a position where you've got a really good flow of deals and investors coming into your business. Now, you may have an occasion, and we have certainly been there before, where we have had the money, and we couldn't get the deals, or we've had the deals, and couldn't get the money, but hey guess what, that's just life, right? However, when you follow our system that we are going to talk you through now, you will get into a position where you've got a good deal flow and a good money flow. Now, depending on what strategy you are doing, there are occasions when we would say focus on the deal first, rather than the money. So, let's explain these to you.

If you are going to do rent to rent, serviced accommodation, and HMOs, you are not going to buy any assets, okay, if you're doing rent to rent, you are going to acquire an existing property from a landlord, and manage it or you're going to become the tenant, and then you're going to use it as a HMO serviced accommodation. Typically, to get a deal like that over the line, the investment required can be as little as two to four thousand pounds, and a rent-to-rent HMO or serviced accommodation unit over say a five-year period could produce you about sixty thousand pounds a year. So think about this, if you are just three thousand pounds away from acquiring an asset that you don't even have to own for that to give you sixty thousand pounds a year, trust me, you will do whatever it takes to get that three thousand pounds, like you will literally call everyone in your phonebook; friends, family members, business associates, or you can go and raise that money on a credit card. So, what we are saying here is to raise a few thousand pounds is not that difficult, if you are determined. When you do rent to rent, think about the money, you will need some money to get the deal over the line. But it's not like you've got to go and raise half a million pounds for a property or a development, and think about it you can probably get that money quite quickly, but in the back of your mind you may be thinking it sounds too easy to be true - just remember before going any further, address your mindset.

If you are wanting to buy property, like single legs or HMOs, or you want to do flips, imagine this, you have found a deal and now today, you're working with an agent, the agent is going to want to know who is buying the property, proof of funds, and going to request that you engage with the solicitor quickly. So, it might be all well and good having an amazing deal, but if you haven't got the money ready, or if you haven't got an investor lined up, then how are you going to complete that purchase? Therefore, in this case you should be spending more time focusing on the money.

If you're doing land development or commercial conversions, it is pretty similar too . You will need to focus on finding investors and raising money, then you can go and put that investor into a deal, but as you grow on the journey, you'll be thinking about deals and money at the same time as your aim will be to get an equal amount coming into the business. We're always looking to raise money for deals, but occasionally, you can look for the deal first as well. Let's say for example, we had a deal on the table today and one of us got on the phone and called the other and said, 'hey I've just come across an amazing commercial conversion, we need to raise half a million pounds. 'Well, we wouldn't not do the deal, we would say to the agent, look, we work with a high network of sophisticated investors, we'd like to put an offer forward.' We are going to then go out to our network, and we're going to look to raise the money. We are quite good at raising money and don't worry you're going to be good at it too. The next step is that we can make a few phone calls, do a few social media posts, put it out to various networks - hence very important to be connected, and we will do whatever it takes to raise that half a million pounds. Hey, if we then couldn't get the money, what is the worst thing that can happen? We would lose the deal and that's just life.

We also have what we call the 'No Money Down Blueprint.' A lot of people think that to build a property business, you need lots of your own cash. Well, look, you do need cash, but there are many strategies that are very low entry levels and even if you're in a position now where you haven't got the cash, let us briefly share one with you.

OPM - OTHER PEOPLE'S MONEY

You can use OPM (other people's money). If you are serious and really do your homework to find great deals, people will invest in the great projects you find. for example, let's say you do not have money for a down payment, but you have a great credit score, a consistent job and income, and you have a friend, family member or know someone who has cash but bad credit, you both could joint venture on a deal. The partnership is good for both because each brings something unique to the table: the individual supplies the cash and you get the mortgage. One critical piece of advice we would give to you is to know your numbers, ensure that you both come to an agreement of the profit percentage division and get it all documented and above board.

YOUR OWN CAPITAL

So, if you've got a bit of cash in the bank, the chances are, it's burning a hole, it's not doing anything, it's going down in value due to inflation which has sky-rocketed for a while now. You know, we believe that you should always have a small amount of cash in the bank for a rainy day. However, having money in a bank is not earning you any interest. for every one hundred thousand pounds that someone has sitting in a bank, every year with inflation, they lose approximately two and a half to three thousand pounds in value. So, what I would recommend is to get your money working for you. And this is something you're going to do and educate your investors about getting their money working for them and you need to show them how you can make that happen.

BRIDGING FINANCE

Bridging finance is a short-term loan, getting you from A to B until you secure a more permanent option. A bridging loan is more expensive, and you may be paying in the region of 1% per month. So that's 12% a year. Plus, you've got some entry and exit fees. So, you could be looking at maybe 14-16% interest over a 12-month period . We have had bridging finance before to do some of our rehab projects in Crewe and Stoke and ended up paying about 14 and a half to 15% over the 12 months. But bridging can be arranged for a short-term period, you'll typically easily get a bridge loan between three and 24 months. And it's really good for refurbishments, auctions and financing some of your developments; the bridging company is going to have what's called first, second or third charge on that property. So, let's give you an example. We bought some HMOs, in Crewe in Stoke, the mortgage company had what's called a first charge. So, if we ever defaulted and never paid the mortgage, they needed to be able to come and claim that property, the first charge enables them to be the first people in line to get paid out when the asset is sold. A bridging company ideally would like the first charge, but in a lot of cases, you already have a charge on an asset, where you're looking to raise some additional funding. So, the bridging company might get a second or third charge, which means they're slightly down the pecking order, and so increases their risk, this is why they typically charge more interest than others. The other reason they charge slightly more is that it's a great opportunity giver for some, especially as they can get money out to you very quickly. You're going to want to pay your bridge off as quickly as possible with a cheaper solution. A company called Shawbrook, does a really nice bridge to let, where they will actually help you purchase the entire product on a bridge, they will give you that free period of time, say three months, allow you to do the refurb and then they'll switch you into one of their mortgage products. We actually did that with one of our JV deals in Ipswich with one of our joint venture partners, we got a bridge to let from Shawbrook Bank and then switched into their commercial products and it worked really well, for us it was a really good solution. So, keep an open mind with bridging. It's also very good for auction properties. Because a lot of the time when you go to auction, and you want to buy a property, say a run down, dirty smelling, ugly house on the street, it's normally not livable, and unless a property is livable, i.e. a kitchen, running water, toilet shower facilities, you can't actually get a mortgage. So, a lot of people use auction bridging finance to take you from point A to point B, you get the bridging finance short term loan, you purchase the property at an auction and get in there to do a quick turnaround on the refurb. After which you then switch to a normal mortgage product. So, again, keep an open mind on bridging, it can work really well. However, also be aware that if you don't pay it back in the timeframe, there can be some real, big penalties.

BRIDGING FINANCE

Bridging finance is a short-term loan, getting you from A to B until you secure a more permanent option. A bridging loan is more expensive, and you may be paying in the region of 1% per month. So that's 12% a year. Plus, you've got some entry and exit fees. So, you could be looking at maybe 14-16% interest over a 12-month period . We have had bridging finance before to do some of our rehab projects in Crewe and Stoke and ended up paying about 14 and a half to 15% over the 12 months. But bridging can be arranged for a short-term period, you'll typically easily get a bridge loan between three and 24 months. And it's really good for refurbishments, auctions and financing some of your developments; the bridging company is going to have what's called first, second or third charge on that property. So, let's give you an example. We bought some HMOs, in Crewe in Stoke, the mortgage company had what's called a first charge. So, if we ever defaulted and never paid the mortgage, they needed to be able to come and claim that property, the first charge enables them to be the first people in line to get paid out when the asset is sold. A bridging company ideally would like the first charge, but in a lot of cases, you already have a charge on an asset, where you're looking to raise some additional funding. So, the bridging company might get a second or third charge, which means they're slightly down the pecking order, and so increases their risk, this is why they typically charge more interest than others. The other reason they charge slightly more is that it's a great opportunity giver for some, especially as they can get money out to you very quickly. You're going to want to pay your bridge off as quickly as possible with a cheaper solution. A company called Shawbrook, does a really nice bridge to let, where they will actually help you purchase the entire product on a bridge, they will give you that free period of time, say three months, allow you to do the refurb and then they'll switch you into one of their mortgage products. We actually did that with one of our JV deals in Ipswich with one of our joint venture partners, we got a bridge to let from Shawbrook Bank and then switched into their commercial products and it worked really well, for us it was a really good solution. So, keep an open mind with bridging. It's also very good for auction properties. Because a lot of the time when you go to auction, and you want to buy a property, say a run down, dirty smelling, ugly house on the street, it's normally not livable, and unless a property is livable, i.e. a kitchen, running water, toilet shower facilities, you can't actually get a mortgage. So, a lot of people use auction bridging finance to take you from point A to point B, you get the bridging finance short term loan, you purchase the property at an auction and get in there to do a quick turnaround on the refurb. After which you then switch to a normal mortgage product. So, again, keep an open mind on bridging, it can work really well. However, also be aware that if you don't pay it back in the timeframe, there can be some real, big penalties.

DEVELOPMENT FUNDING

We are now going to have a quick look at development funding. Possibly some of you are already property investors, you've done some rent-to-rent, single lets, HMOs and maybe you are at the point where you don't want to bother with single lets anymore, you want to go into doing land deals and commercial conversions. Now, one of the great things about us and Assets for Life is that we are always looking for our next business partner. We love doing joint ventures with our graduates, people that we work with on our training programs, people that we really get to know when they join the Assets for Life Academy, which is our yearlong mentoring mastermind, hand holding accountability program. This is where we really take you through the entire process and hold your hand to ensure that you get the results that you want. Now, when you start doing bigger deals, and go out to the development funders, they will want you to have some type of experience. So, when we first started doing developments, we had no experience, like there's no way we would have got the development funding but because one of us (Jay) was a chartered civil engineer, he'd worked on some of the biggest builds in London, and so the knowledge of project management and building was in the bag, so we were able to get the funding. So, you might need to do your first one or two developments, depending on how big it is, and if possible, team up with an existing developer, where you can then get the funding, share the profits, do the deal together and make money together that way and to be honest with you, it's a lot more fun doing it with someone else than doing it on your own. So, development funding is a loan facility that goes towards the purchase of a land or development deal. There's a range of funding companies and options available; we would recommend that you use a commercial funding broker that has access to all of the commercial lenders. Typically speaking, the commercial funder will lend 50% of the land purchase and 70% of the development costs, you may then need to find in the region of 20 to 30% as your equity piece and the development funder will have first charge. Let us just show you a quick example. Right. So, let's say you find a piece of land and it's 100,000 pounds to purchase and the construction costs are half a million pounds. Well, the development funder may give you £50,000 pounds towards the purchase price and £350,000 towards the development cost. So that's £400,000 they will give you, which means you will need to find £200,000 as the equity piece to show the development funders that you have got skin in the game. Now where can you get that money from? You're either going to get it from your own bank account, or you're going to go into a joint venture with investors. And later in this module, we are going to show you exactly how to raise these funds. And wherever possible, we always look to use investor money and this is pretty much the worst-case scenario. Whenever as business partners we have our exciting telephone conversations when we have just found another deal and had the offer accepted. Either one will say okay that is really good, what is the cost? The response might be total cost purchase price plus the refurb, or the new build costs and all the legal fees. Let's say we're in for a million quid, in our heads, we think ok right how much do we need for investors? So, in that example, it may be 20%, we will just think right, we need to find £200,000, in some cases, we might need to find a bit more, but we are going to be there or thereabouts.

When it comes to our development sites, we use development funders, where you can go and raise money, they've got access to thousands of investors, and can raise money for your developments fast. They are constantly looking for new deals, there's a simple application process, about four to five weeks for approval, you find the deal, they find the money, you basically can scale up quick, once the Trust has been built. So, it's more of a personal service, you won't necessarily get the best rates in town, but you can potentially get the money quickly. And if you're a newer type developer, then they're more open to work with you. If you go to someone like Lloyds commercial, you'll get a much better rate. But the whole process might take 12-16 weeks. If you're a new developer, however, they might not take that too kindly and may just show you the door. So again, like mortgages and bridging funding when it comes to development funding, there are lots of development funding options available. You have to go and hunt the marketplace using a commercial broker and find the best deal that you can get.

Ultimately keep an open mind about bringing in a more experienced developer that can join you so that it can be easier for you to get that funding. And you can get a better rate for development funding. We absolutely love one of our latest developments. We received about four and a half million pounds from the development funders at about 7%. That is cheap money and by doing this, you're really able to scale and you can also do multiple developments at any one time.

JOINT VENTURES

There are so many of our Academy members that are now raising joint venture funding so let's dive into it a little. We would like to take this time to re-emphasise what we mentioned in chapter one; confidence and mindset are very important, especially when you start to venture out to raise money, everything will change for you when you get this right. The old saying that "two heads are better than one" describes the value of a property joint venture very well. A joint venture is simply when two or more people collaborate, bringing their skills and resources together, to complete a project or create a property business.

So, what is a joint venture?

A joint venture (JV) is a business arrangement in which two or more parties agree to pool their resources for the purpose of accomplishing a specific task. So, let's have a look at why people will JV with you. Now, we don't know about you or where you are at, but maybe you were thinking or are thinking like we did five years ago, Who the hell's going to give us cash? One of us had lost a renewable energy business and was in debt of minus 392,000 pounds, and the first-time round in property, lost over 2 million pounds in that property portfolio, we did everything you shouldn't do, with no training and mentoring. What a big mistake that was to not have a mentor, and to not be part of an Academy that was going to help us go from where we were to where we wanted to go. This is why having support helps. Mentoring is absolutely essential for your property business success. So, we went into this being unsure, asking ourselves, can we really do this?

But let's have a look at all of the reasons why someone is going to joint venture with you, you have now got the best education. And you can say to your investors, "I've been trained, I understand what I'm doing. I'm part of a fantastic network called Assets for Life." You have got this system that people don't have, and they don't understand that property freedom formula is the seven step system that you need to follow and implement, which will enable you to get the property deals. You're also part of a winning team. That's a really big tick when it comes to investors. And I want to be clear, now, investors are not looking for you to have lots of property deals, investors are not looking for you to be some big property guru, what investors are looking for, is to know you, like you, trust you, and make sure that you've got the right support systems and processes in place. And ultimately, they're looking for you to have passion. They're looking for you to have enthusiasm. They want you to have the core knowledge and you're going to get out there soon, you're going to know what's going on in Colchester or Birmingham or Chelmsford, Newcastle or wherever you are at, in the UK. And you are going to have the time. And I know lots of you are just starting five to seven hours a week, low interest rates. Another great reason why investors are going to invest with you is because you can get some great property deals, terrible pensions, and the stock market is risky, not a good place to have the cash. It's exciting to JV with you when you've got the winning deals, and ultimately investors are going to invest in you because it's YOU. You've got to take the investors on a journey, they need to know you, like you and trust you. I can guarantee that when you get that first or next investor over the line, your confidence is going to skyrocket. And then what's really important is that you service that investor, you do exactly what you said you were going to do, you build that relationship. So, when the investor comes to the end of their term, guess what they're going to do? They're going to invest with you again. We currently have six million pounds in the pool at the moment and we just keep recycling this six million and adding to it. Just last weekend, one of my investors reinvested into his third year £227,000, that was the value at the end of year two. Now, another good question to ask yourself and to understand is why do you actually want to do the Joint Ventures? Okay, now, I don't know about you or where you're at but maybe you are in a similar position to where we were a few years ago, when we started this process. We didn't have access to a big pot of cash, yet we were still able to build a property business by using joint venture finance. So, let's have a look. Number one, you have no money to invest. And, if your back is against it right now and you are not in the best financial position, we are here to tell you this is not a get rich quick scheme. It is not hit a button and you're going to become a millionaire, that doesn't exist. It's a steady process that does take effort to achieve success, if you get the chance to secure a place in our Academy and go through the training along with our hand holding mentoring program, and you throw yourself into this, even if it's just part time, we can promise you, you will be surprised at how possible this is. You're going to start firstly by doing 'No Money Down Deals. And what we mean by this is that you are not going to use any of your own money. That's really scalable, because it doesn't matter who you are and how rich you are. You have to keep in mind that there is the possibility that you are going to run out of money at some point if we tie it up in property deals. Even Alan Sugar, who invests in billions of pounds worth of property, does joint venture funding, he goes and finds investors. Here is the thing, you get to work as part of a team and can scale much quicker. You get an endless supply of cash, as well as reduce your risk, and you get to help change people's lives, an infinite return for you. I don't know about you, but we would much prefer 50% of something than 100% nothing. Wouldn't you agree? We are not greedy, it is way better to share the love, share the workload and share the profits. We would much prefer to have multiple deals going on where we get a bit from this and a bit from that whilst doing less work, getting multiple deals using none of our own money, that's how you start to earn more cash. Ultimately, it is fun to do Joint Ventures, we spend a lot of time with our families, going go karting, clay pigeon shooting, hanging out, nice dinner, spa days, trips into London, you know, it's a lot of fun. Now I (Liam) don't particularly like golf, I'm absolutely useless at golf. But I have gone to Top Golf in Chigwell a couple of times with potential investors, why? Because we will go and do what investors like to do in order to find a common ground, and the sooner you can find some common ground with an investor, the sooner you've got a connection, once you've got that connection, they are more likely to invest in you, because that's how they get to know, like and trust you. This is one of the best tips we have got for you - find some common ground with an investor.

A joint venture for property investment could be between anybody, but here are some examples where skill or resource gaps can be filled with a joint venture;

- A family venture, where the son and/or daughter has

construction skills and the mum and/or dad has the funds or grandparents that have a little something tucked away that they saved for their grandchildren to go and invest.

- A builder, architect and estate agent get together to pool funds and skills.
- Property investors who are time poor can come together to share the workload.

There are many more examples but essentially all joint venture teams will have members who can either bring the funds required, meet the time demands and have the skills and expertise necessary.

A property joint venture has to work for all the parties involved. A joint venture is only a good solution if it delivers financially beneficial results and if the process is smooth enough.

Some things to remember when going into Joint Ventures

1. Write down clearly what each person will do i.e. what jobs & responsibilities will they each undertake?
2. Agree on the % split of profit or fixed interest rate %.
3. Decide on which structure to use, either profit share or fixed interest rate, as this is dependent on individual's needs.
4. Another major point on the agenda must be how the property is to be secured. That means, who is going to be the legal owner of the property and below are examples;

- Create a special company to buy the property and deal with all finance through that business. That company is known as an SPV (Special Purpose Vehicle).
- Both/All members can buy the property in both/all names.
- One member buys the property and the other/s has legal charge over it.

In the case of setting up an SPV (Special Purpose Vehicle) all the members can become shareholders of the business and this is a good way of dealing with profit share. Setting up an SPV is very common.

Lastly, there may be sufficient trust, that means one or more members of the joint venture have no legal right to the property i.e. they are completely unsecured. It really all depends on what suits the members best, and often their individual tax situation.

Investing in property as we have mentioned before can be very challenging, especially if you do not know what you are doing and things can go wrong at the best of times, so when you also factor in the human element it becomes even more of a minefield.

Here are some of our recommendations to help you sail smoothly;

- Make the goals and exit plans very clear in a written agreement.
- Don't just jump into property investment through a joint venture without guidance or mentoring, get some experience with the right support as this will also enable you to have a good track record of doing deals on your own.
- Discuss what you'll do in the bad scenarios when a project fails or a deal falls through.
- Get yourself a mentor.
- Have a good solicitor and accountant to hand.

The most important stage of a joint venture agreement is right at the start. It's vital that you and your new business partner/s know each other well, build that rapport as we mentioned earlier by finding a common ground.

MORTGAGES

Mortgages come in various types, but challenges like bad credit or lack of credentials can hinder access. A JV partnership can help—one partner with good credit acts as a mortgage host, becoming the company director while the other is a shareholder. After six months, the shareholder can become a director, building credit and enabling future mortgage access.

Now, in relation to mortgages, we are not mortgage brokers. So we highly recommend that you seek out independent advice, either through your independent financial adviser, or you use a specialist broker. We have some really fantastic people in house to hand that we normally recommend to our clients and we have access to over 144 lenders.

So, let's have a look at what a mortgage is - A mortgage is a legal agreement by which a bank or building society lends money at interest in exchange for taking title of the debtor's property, you can go and get a fixed rate or variable rate mortgage, and you can use a broker to shop around for the best deals. We do not recommend that you start walking into all your High Street banks, yes High Street banks can be really good for residential mortgages. However, when it comes to investment mortgages, you'll typically find they don't have the best options.

for instance, we have got some brokers that purely focus on finding us companies that will lend money for development funding, then we've got a broker who is really good for single let type products and others for HMOs and other commercial type lenders. Typically, the bank will lend you 75% loan to value (LTV) and you have to go and find 25% as the initial down payment. If you don't have that money, you can always do a 50/50 JV with an investor where they put in the money and you do the work.

Fixed vs Variable

With a fixed-rate mortgage, it means that the rates and payments are lower, a higher percentage of money being approved can happen. There's no need to refinance to take advantage of lower rates. After the introductory term ends, rates can increase steeply so you need to keep an eye on that. You have adjustable-rate mortgages, where the rates and payments are lower, a higher percentage barring being approved, so you can potentially get more money, there's no need to refinance and take advantage of lower interest rates. However, be very careful as you might get an introductory term of, say, two years. This is a really low interest rate, but after two years, it will increase really fast, and you're going to need to switch into a new deal and it can be a little bit more complicated. So, a few things for you to be aware of, we would always be taking advice from our broker. We would always be looking at the market at the time of getting the mortgage. We are not saying that we are definitely correct about getting more fixed rate mortgages. Some people prefer to have adjustable-rate mortgages, but for us as property investors, we just like to know where we stand every month with our HMOs. Especially due to the fact that we do a lot of HMOs.

Interest-only mortgages have lower payments as you only pay the interest, leaving the principal due at the end. These suit investors aiming for high cash flow, hoping inflation and property value growth will erode the debt.

Repayment mortgages gradually clear the principal, ensuring full repayment by term end but with higher payments. Investors may shift to lower leverage and repayment focus as they age. Preferences depend on goals and life stage.

To truly understand the power of creative funding and strategic thinking in property investment, let's take a look at Alan Edwards' journey. Alan, a seasoned professional in the property and construction industry, faced significant challenges during the financial meltdown in the UK during the 1990s. Despite his extensive experience and ambition, the lack of support from traditional banks forced him to continue in his corporate role instead of pursuing property development full-time. However, Alan's determination never wavered. Through the mentorship and guidance provided by AFL, Alan has been able to leverage his deep industry knowledge and apply innovative funding strategies, such as vendor finance and purchase lease options, to significantly expand his property portfolio.

Alan's story is a testament to the importance of not just understanding traditional funding methods, but also embracing creative financial strategies to overcome obstacles and seize opportunities. Today, Alan is not only a full-time property investor and developer, but he is also building an international group of companies centred around property investment and education. His journey illustrates how, with the right mindset and approach to funding, you can turn financial challenges into opportunities for growth and success. You can find out more about Alan's impressive achievements and his strategic approach in the final chapter of this book.

To conclude, understanding and choosing the right funding strategy is crucial for your success in property investment. Whether it's making savvy use of other people's money, navigating the complexities of bridging finance, or securing development funding, the key is to stay informed and proactive. Remember, each investment scenario is unique, and the best funding path depends on your specific goals, resources, and the market conditions. Armed with the knowledge from this chapter, you are better prepared to make informed decisions that align with your investment strategy and drive your property business towards greater profitability and success.

Assignment

Funding Strategy Workbook

- **Funding Review:** List out all potential funding options available to you, as described in this chapter. Next to each, note any contacts or resources you have that could help you access these options, such as potential investors, financial institutions, or brokers.
- **Scenario Planning:** Create hypothetical scenarios for each type of funding. for example, outline a plan for how you would secure a bridging loan for a quick refurbishment project or how you would pitch to a potential joint venture partner. Include potential challenges and how you might overcome them.
- **Network Expansion:** Identify and list down at least three networking actions you can take to expand your contacts in the financial sector. This could be attending property investment webinars, joining local real estate investment groups, or setting up meetings with financial advisors.
- **Documentation Preparation:** Prepare a template for a funding proposal that you could use to present a project to potential investors or lenders. Include key elements such as the project summary, expected returns, risk analysis, and your background.

This assignment aims to deepen your understanding of different funding mechanisms and prepares you to apply these concepts in real-world investing scenarios. By actively engaging with the material and planning how to use these funding strategies, you set the foundation for successful property investment ventures.

CHAPTER THREE
SITE FINDINGS

The Portfolio Matrix

Site findings in the property market in the UK refers to the process of conducting research and gathering information about specific locations or properties for analysis and decision-making purposes. As Jay says in his book Property Metamorphosis , "Every single postcode is a micro-economy" This involves investigating various factors such as employment sources, schools, climate, desirable size units, topography, local amenities, transportation links, civil infrastructure and market conditions about the property or development site. Site findings provide valuable insights to help property developers, investors, and professionals make informed decisions about property purchases, developments, and investments. It enables them to assess the potential suitability, opportunities, and constraints associated with a particular site, allowing for strategic planning and maximising the value and potential of the property in the market. These findings are crucial in facilitating informed choices and mitigating risks when entering the UK property market.

Let's look closely at the property portfolio matrix, which comprises some of the UK's most popular property strategies. It is essential to note that you do not have to start from the lower levels to advance to the higher levels. Our graduates have initiated their careers in commercial conversions and land development projects, to name a few.

Throughout this section, what's important is to figure out your interests, what suits you best, and which strategy will likely have the most significant impact on your life in the shortest time possible. All these techniques are phenomenal, but it's impossible to apply all of them at once, as it would leave you burnt out and demotivated. Therefore, it is crucial to get laser-focused on a specific strategy and make it your priority. So, in the portfolio matrix, we have rent-to-rent HMOs and serviced accommodation. Deal packaging is another excellent method to begin.

Moving ahead in the matrix, you have an opportunity to explore lease options, buy now and pay later. Some of you, however, might be interested in getting involved in buying and selling properties where you can add value and generate substantial profits, which is known as flipping.

Or, you prefer to purchase property assets that you could convert into single-let properties or HMOs. On the other hand, if you're seeking a more significant venture, you might want to go straight into commercial conversions or land development deals.

This section will delve into the property types you should secure, how to identify these projects, and where to find the most lucrative opportunities. Remember, it's crucial to determine what works best for you, stay motivated, and remain focused on making the right investment decisions. Perhaps you'll jump straight into commercial conversions and land development deals. In this section, we will thoroughly explore the types of properties you should secure, where to find these deals, and how to acquire them.

Now, let's discuss the key to success in this endeavour. The properties you should be looking for encompass a wide range of options. They include residential houses, commercial premises, offices, pubs, clubs, care homes, land (with and without planning permission), extensive gardens, and flats. Rental properties are also pertinent if you intend to pursue the rent-to-rent strategy. We will introduce you to each strategy on the property portfolio matrix. We will examine each approach's advantages and disadvantages, providing an honest and unbiased perspective. It will be your task to evaluate and decide which strategy aligns best with your goals and ambitions. You may choose one strategy as your primary focus and another as a secondary approach.

We aim to help you build multiple property income streams using various sources. Diversification is a crucial principle we believe in. It's essential not to put all your eggs in one basket. for instance, we have completed over 54 property deals in the past five years, and we wouldn't want all 54 to consist solely of rent-to-rent serviced accommodation units. Having multiple income streams and engaging in diverse property deals is vital for long-term success.

THE PROPERTY **Portfolio Matrix**

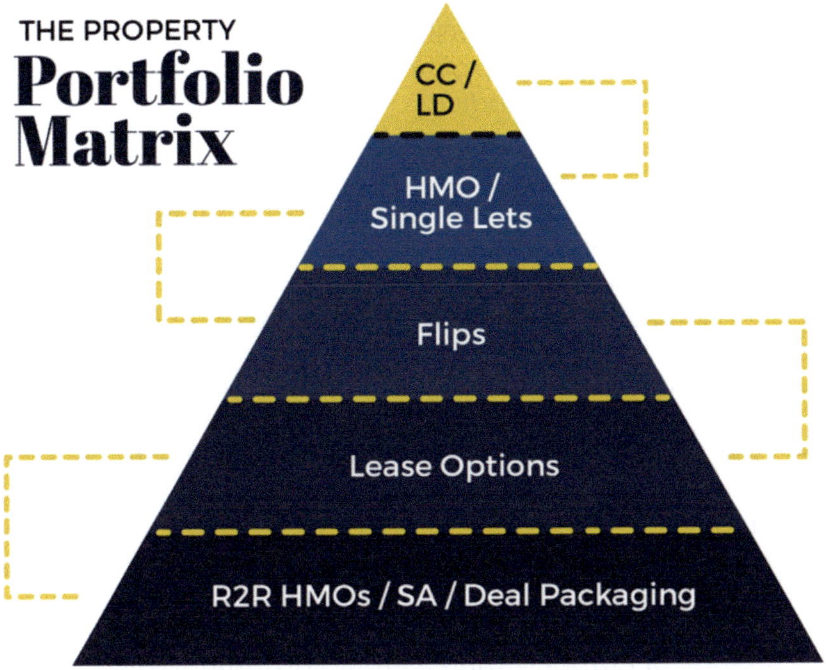

So, let us delve deeper into each strategy outlined in the portfolio matrix. Prepare for an exciting journey as you decide which path to embark on.

Rent-to-Rent

Rent-to-rent is a property strategy offering a high cash-flowing income model without significant deposits or outright property purchases, making it an attractive option for individuals with limited capital or poor credit history. This strategy involves renting a property from a landlord and then subletting it, typically as a House in Multiple Occupation (HMO) or serviced accommodation.

One of the critical benefits of rent-to-rent is its potential for quick profitability. Substantial profits can be generated with proper management and efficient systems, typically ranging from £500 to £1,000 monthly net per property. The low upfront capital requirement, often between £3,000 and £5,000, makes this strategy accessible to many, including those with minimal savings.

Rent-to-rent offers flexibility as agreements are generally shorter than traditional property ownership; this enables quick adaptation to market demands and the exploration of different property sectors. Negotiating directly with landlords and building trust can lead to favourable rental agreements, bypassing intermediaries.

Scaling a rent-to-rent business is relatively straightforward once successful systems and processes are established. This scalability allows for the creation of multiple income streams from various properties. However, it is crucial to understand and comply with the rules and regulations governing rent-to-rent agreements to avoid legal issues and potential financial or reputational damage.

Another advantage of rent-to-rent is the opportunity for long-term partnerships and collaborations. Building relationships with landlords, tenants, and fellow investors can open doors to joint ventures and partnerships, further enhancing profitability and providing a support network.

Regarding market demand, rent-to-rent can cater to different segments, such as house sharing, HMOs or providing serviced accommodation for short-term guests. This versatility ensures a steady stream of tenants or guests, increasing the profitability of your rent-to-rent business.

While rent-to-rent has challenges, such as diligent property management and regulatory compliance, it offers a low-risk entry point into property investment. It allows for learning and gaining valuable experience in the property market, acquiring skills transferable to future investments.

In summary, rent-to-rent is a viable and profitable strategy for those entering the property market. It provides high cash flow, flexibility, and scalability. With thorough research, proper planning, and adherence to regulations, rent-to-rent can be a lucrative avenue for property investment and income generation.

Serviced Accommodation

In the previous section, we discussed the concept of rent-to-rent, which allows you to use properties as serviced accommodation.

Whether you have an existing flat or house, it may be worth considering a slight change in strategy and exploring the benefits of offering serviced accommodation.

Serviced accommodation refers to fully furnished apartments or houses available for short-term and long-term stays. These accommodations include all utility bills and provide hotel-like amenities. Guests are charged per night, week, or month, and you can charge per guest without needing an Assured Shorthold Tenancy Agreement. This setup is similar to hotel accommodation, eliminating many challenges associated with traditional tenant-landlord relationships.

By opting for serviced accommodation, you can avoid issues commonly faced by landlords, such as tenants not paying rent or difficulties in eviction. With rent-to-rent serviced accommodation, you receive payment at the time of booking, typically through credit card transactions. This allows for immediate cash flow and potentially higher returns than traditional single-let properties or houses in multiple occupations (HMOs).

To find bookings for your serviced accommodation, you can utilise platforms like booking.com or Airbnb, attracting guests with different budgets and preferences. Your potential guest pool includes mid-range budget travellers, luxury seekers, business professionals, contractors, tradespeople, holidaymakers, families, tourists, and individuals on short business trips. The market for serviced accommodation is substantial and is currently one of the fastest-growing property strategies in the UK.

One of the significant advantages of operating serviced accommodation is the potential for a systemised and hands-off business. Cleaning companies can handle the turnover process between guests, and you can provide self-check-in options using key boxes or critical codes. By implementing these streamlined systems, you can free up your time and focus on scaling your serviced accommodation business.

Two-bedroom apartments are often the preferred choice in many areas when searching for properties suitable for serviced accommodation. These apartments, particularly in newly built complexes, require minimal work to get started. You can negotiate rent-to-rent agreements or consider purchasing houses or flats. The goal is to minimise cash investment and maximise profits.

Serviced accommodation presents a fantastic opportunity for high cash flow and scalability. Many successful property investors have embraced this strategy, as it allows for both hands-on and hands-off management approaches. Consider converting your existing flat, even if it currently generates a net profit of £200 as a single let, as it can make five or six times that amount as serviced accommodation.

Overall, serviced accommodation is a compelling property strategy offering various benefits. With the increasing demand for home-like stays rather than hotels, there is ample opportunity to provide attractive accommodations to travellers. So, explore the potential of serviced accommodation and discover how it can generate substantial profits while giving you a flexible and hands-on or hands-off property investment option.

In addition to the financial benefits of serviced accommodation, it's essential to consider this strategy's flexibility and scalability. With serviced accommodation, you can adapt the business model to suit your preferences and goals. Whether you prefer a more hands-on approach, overseeing the day-to-day operations, or a hands-off approach, delegating tasks to property management companies, the choice is yours.

One of the key advantages of serviced accommodation is the ability to cater to various types of guests. By providing a range of amenities and services, you can attract a diverse clientele, from short-term vacationers to long-term business travellers. This versatility allows you to maximise occupancy rates throughout the year, ensuring a steady income stream.

Moreover, the demand for serviced accommodation is more comprehensive than a specific demographic or location. As more travellers seek alternative accommodation options that offer the comforts of home, the market for serviced accommodation continues to expand. This presents an exciting opportunity for property investors to capitalise on this growing trend and establish a successful business in the hospitality sector.

Furthermore, operating serviced accommodation can open up opportunities for strategic partnerships and collaborations. By networking with local businesses, tourism organisations, and corporate entities, you can establish mutually beneficial relationships that drive bookings and increase your property's visibility. Leveraging these connections can help you attract high-value guests and secure long-term bookings, enhancing the profitability of your serviced accommodation business.

It's important to note that successful serviced accommodation businesses are built on a foundation of exceptional guest experiences. By providing top-notch customer service, maintaining the cleanliness and functionality of your properties, and addressing any issues promptly, you can cultivate a loyal customer base and receive positive reviews and feedback. These satisfied guests are more likely to return for future stays and recommend your accommodations to others, contributing to the long-term success of your serviced accommodation venture.

In conclusion, serviced accommodation offers a lucrative opportunity for property investors to generate substantial income, build a scalable business, and provide value-added services to travellers. By embracing this fast-growing property strategy, you can tap into a thriving market, create memorable guest experiences, and achieve financial success in the hospitality industry. Whether you're a seasoned investor or a novice in the real estate sector, exploring the potential of serviced accommodation can lead to a rewarding and profitable investment journey.

Deal Packaging

Let's delve into deal packaging and explore its potential within the property market. Deal packaging is a process where you identify and secure profitable property deals, and then sell them to other investors for a fee. This offers a unique opportunity to discover and sell lucrative deals, making it one of the most valuable aspects of property investment. However, despite its significance, many individuals need help with deal packaging due to time constraints.

Even as experienced investors, we have personally purchased deals from deal finders , highlighting the potential for anyone, including you, to become a proficient deal packager. This isn't just about earning a substantial income, it's about the potential for personal growth and financial success. By sourcing rent-to-rent opportunities, single-let HMOs, or small flips for other investors, you can start small and grow your business at your own pace. As you progress in your deal packaging journey, you may explore more significant ventures such as land development and commercial conversions. These deals have the potential for substantial financial gains, often commanding a sourcing fee ranging from 1% to 3% of the purchase price. for example, if you successfully source a land development opportunity worth a million pounds, a 2% sourcing fee would accumulate to twenty thousand pounds.

fortunately, deal packaging requires minimal upfront cash investment. The key to deal packaging success is ensuring your compliance with industry regulations. But what's truly empowering is the scalability of this income stream. You can choose the number of deals you wish to source and increase your earning potential. This flexibility means that you can start small and grow your business at your own pace. Furthermore, deal packaging allows you to accumulate substantial funds to be used as deposits for your property purchases, giving you even more control over your financial future.

Deal packaging presents a fascinating and profitable avenue in the property market. By honing your skills as a successful deal finder and packager, you have the potential to generate significant income while building a solid foundation for your personal property portfolio. This isn't just a possibility, it's a promise. With the right knowledge and strategies, you can confidently navigate the property market and succeed in deal packaging.

If you need to utilise joint venture funds or prefer a combination of strategies, deal packaging offers a fantastic opportunity to enter the property market and earn considerable sums. Deal packaging can generate substantial income by locating investors and meeting their needs. Some investors may require you to source and project manage properties, while others may prefer a turnkey solution where you handle everything from sourcing and project management to tenant management.

When dealing with investors, securing an initial commitment fee from them is crucial. for example, if you were our investor and wanted us to source deals for you, you'd be required to pay a deposit to initiate the process. This not only starts a fruitful partnership but also cements a mutual commitment to success, ensuring that we dedicate our expertise and resources to finding the perfect properties that meet your needs. Let's say you agree to this arrangement, and we start the process. It may take up to 90 days to find suitable properties and request an activation fee of two thousand pounds, which is refundable. This fee activates our team and us, and we will begin sourcing based on your criteria. Once you are satisfied with the property, you can pay the remaining balance and proceed with the deal. We would only source properties for those who have paid a refundable deposit, as this establishes trust and commitment from both parties.

This approach is an excellent way to embark on your property journey and establish relationships in the industry. Additionally, consider this as an additional income stream. If you cannot execute all the deals yourself, you can sell some of them.

It's important to note that deal packaging, like any investment strategy, comes with its own set of risks and challenges. It does not involve property ownership, so it's not a wealth-creation strategy. It may also not provide passive income as money will not flow automatically. However, deal packaging can be a viable option if you're looking to address any current financial challenges or generate a significant part-time income. Imagine sourcing one deal per month at five thousand pounds per deal, resulting in twelve deals per year, equating to sixty thousand pounds annually.

Deal packaging involves using platforms such as Rightmove, making phone calls, attending property viewings, and building relationships. It's a lucrative business that can outperform your current income. Maintain an open mind regarding deal packaging, as it offers a valuable income stream to enhance your property portfolio. Trudy Searly, one of our graduates made 10,000 from packaging her first two deals.

Lease Option

Lease options are an option structure where you agree to purchase a property at a set price, but you have the flexibility to pay for it later. It's essentially a "buy now, pay later" arrangement. With a lease option, you typically have four to five years to exercise your option to buy the property. To activate the option, you usually pay a nominal amount, such as one pound, but your solicitor will guide you through the process.

At the end of the option term, you have several choices. You can return the property, execute the option, buy the property, or sell the option to another investor though the selling of the option must take place during the option term. It's important to note that a lease option is an option, not an obligation, so you can walk away from the deal if you choose.

Lease options work best with motivated sellers. You can identify motivated sellers by looking for properties that have been on the market for an extended period, such as three months, six months, or even a year. In these cases, the sellers are usually highly motivated to sell. You can approach them and propose a lease option where you agree to buy their property at an agreed-upon price, but you won't exercise the option for several years. In the meantime, you pay them rent to help cover their mortgage payments. This allows you to lease the property and convert it into a cash-generating asset like an HMO or a single let.

One of the significant financial benefits of lease options is that the rent you pay can sometimes be used as a down payment towards the property's purchase price. for instance, if you pay five hundred pounds per month in rent, that's six thousand pounds per year. Over a five-year lease option, you would have accumulated thirty thousand pounds, which can be used as a down payment towards the agreed-upon purchase price. This can significantly reduce your initial investment and be a game-changer when it comes time to secure financing or use joint venture finance.

Another advantage of lease options is that property prices appreciate over time. If you agree to a purchase price of one hundred thousand today, the property may be worth one hundred and twenty or even one hundred and fifty in five years. This means that exercising the option allows you to lock in the equity and potentially benefit from the increase in property value.

Lease options can be a great way to acquire properties without much cash upfront. They allow you to build up equity over time and generate money through rental income. Keeping an open mind and exploring lease options can be a powerful strategy in your property investment journey.

Lease options present a unique opportunity for investors to acquire properties and potentially benefit from increases in property value over time. One of the key advantages of lease options is their flexibility and the potential for creative deal structuring. By utilising lease options, investors can gain access to properties without requiring a significant initial cash outlay, making it a more accessible entry point into the real estate market.

Moreover, lease options foster a win-win situation for investors and property owners. for the investor, it offers the potential to build up equity in a property over time while generating rental income. On the other hand, for property owners, a lease option provides a solution for selling their property, especially if they are struggling to find a buyer in a slow market or facing financial constraints. This mutual benefit underscores the fairness and viability of lease options as a property investment strategy.

Furthermore, lease options empower investors to control a property without immediately assuming all ownership responsibilities. This allows them to thoroughly assess the property, make necessary improvements, and potentially increase its value before deciding whether to exercise the option to purchase it.

Another compelling aspect of lease options is the potential for substantial returns on investment. If the property value appreciates during the option period, the investor can secure the property at a lower price than its market value at the time of the agreement. This creates a lucrative opportunity for profit when the property is sold or refinanced.

Moreover, lease options can be a valuable strategy for diversifying a real estate portfolio and mitigating risks. By entering into lease option agreements on multiple properties, investors can spread their investments across different market segments and locations, reducing the impact of market fluctuations on their overall portfolio. In conclusion, lease options offer a flexible and strategic approach to property investment, allowing investors to leverage their resources and capitalise on market opportunities. By understanding the intricacies of lease options and mastering the art of deal structuring, investors can unlock a wealth of potential in the real estate market.

Flips

Flips are a lucrative method of making money in the UK property market. It involves buying, refurbishing, and selling properties to generate substantial profits. The key is to focus on purchasing distressed properties in desirable locations. The property's value is significantly increased by investing in renovations such as new bedrooms, garden improvements, kitchen upgrades, bathroom renovations, and even extensions or loft conversions. The goal is a return of three times the initial investment, meaning a twenty thousand pounds refurbishment should add around sixty thousand pounds in value.

Flips are attractive to investors as they offer profit-sharing opportunities. Investors can provide the funds while you handle the work, and profits can be split evenly (50/50). Alternatively, you can secure fixed-rate loans from multiple investors, allowing you to retain 100% of the profits after deducting debt servicing costs. Targeting a minimum profit of thirty thousand pounds per flip is crucial to make it worth your time and effort.

Auctions can be an excellent source for finding potential flip properties, although caution is necessary. Set a maximum budget before attending an auction and refrain from emotional bidding. You can undertake numerous flips throughout the year, building a reliable team of builders and establishing connections with favourable estate agents and auction houses. This network can give you better deals before they hit the market. However, gaining these advantages is vital to earn trust and a good reputation.

While flips can be profitable, it is wise to consider other strategies, such as buy-refurbish-refinance (BRR), to retain long-term assets and benefit from rental income and property appreciation. Ultimately, the choice depends on your preferences and investment goals. Creativity plays a crucial role in finding opportunities to add value. for instance, converting one-bedroom flats into two-bedroom flats can significantly increase property value. The same principle applies to transforming three-bedroom properties into four-bedroom or even five-bedroom houses. Learning about what works and is in demand in your local area will help you identify the best value-adding strategies.

Flips can be an excellent way to generate a quick influx of cash into your property portfolio. However, the process of buying, refurbishing, and selling properties requires a significant amount of effort, attention to detail, and risk management skills. A successful flip is not just about the purchase price and refurbishment costs but also factors such as location, potential rental income, and market trends. One essential aspect of flipping is timing. The ideal time to flip a property is when the market is hot and demand exceeds supply. This situation creates a bidding war that can drive up property prices, translating to higher profits for the flipper. It is also necessary to ensure the property is sold at the right time, avoiding holding it for too long, as this will reduce your profits.

Another critical factor in successful flips is understanding your target audience. Consider their preferences and priorities, such as schools, access to public transport, neighbourhood amenities, and other factors that impact their buying decisions. A well-informed understanding of your target audience can help you identify the features that will add the most value to your property.

It is also essential to manage the refurbishment process efficiently. This task involves coordinating various contractors, scheduling the work, and ensuring that the project stays within set timelines and budgets. Timing is critical when managing a refurbishment, as missed deadlines can delay the entire project, ultimately reducing your potential profits.

Marketing your flipped property effectively is crucial to its success. Utilise various channels, such as social media, online classifieds, open houses, and agent referrals, to reach potential buyers effectively. Ensure that your marketing pitch highlights the property's unique features, upgrades, and benefits, making it more attractive to potential buyers.

In conclusion, flips can be an excellent means of generating profits in the UK property market. The key to a successful flip is to purchase the right property in a desirable location, add significant value through renovations, understand the target audience, and market it appropriately. If done well, flipping can be a highly lucrative investment strategy that can lead to substantial returns on investment.

Single Lets

When building a property portfolio, we recommend buying, refurbishing, refinancing, and keeping the assets. Why? When you hold the properties in your portfolio, they become part of your legacy plan, not only an asset for life but something you can pass down to your loved ones. Property values tend to double in many parts of the UK (Particularly the south) every ten years, making it a smart long-term wealth creation strategy.

Understand us; we also appreciate deal packaging and rent-to-rent strategies. They have their merits. But with single lets, you can own the assets, and that's where the actual wealth building begins. So, how do you do it?

The key is to follow the buy, refurbish, refinance and rent approach. You want to purchase properties in a good location at a low price, add value through refurbishments, and then refinance, aiming to recoup as much of your initial deposit and refurbishment costs as possible. This is how you can get houses for free. You have a great deal if you can refinance and get your money back within three years through rental income.

With single lets, you can expect to generate a steady net profit of four hundred to eight hundred pounds per month (market permitting). The beauty of single lets is their stability. Tenants tend to stay for a long time, making it their long-term residential property. This provides you with a reliable and stable rental income for years, unlike HMOs, which may have a high turnover of tenants.

In addition to the steady rental income, Single Lets also significantly offers the potential for good capital growth if you invest in the right areas. Every single postcode is a micro-economy. This becomes an integral part of your legacy-building strategy. Of course, different parts of the UK may offer varying levels of capital growth and yields. We prefer investing in areas with good capital growth and solid yields. We want the values of our properties to increase continually.

Let us share an inspiring success story with you. Julie, one of our Academy members, and her husband, Alex, focused on buy-to-let properties in London. Thanks to the strategies they've learned from our Academy, they recently purchased a property for Two hundred and seventy-four thousand pounds. After a short period, the property was valued at four hundred & twenty-five thousand, representing an increase of one hundred & fifty-one thousand pounds. Julie and Alex will refinance the property, pull out their initial investment capital, and continue renting it out to tenants. They now have the cash flow and their initial investment back to go and pursue another property deal. This success story is a testament to the potential financial growth and success that can be achieved through single lets.

So, consider single lets a fantastic way to start the property investment game. They offer great rates of scale and a solid strategy for using the buy, refurbish, refinance approach. It's a path towards long-term wealth creation and building a legacy.

Houses In Multiple Occupations

This section will discuss Houses in Multiple Occupations (HMOs). An HMO is a property where at least three tenants live, forming more than one household, and share facilities like toilets, bathrooms, or kitchens. HMOs can be a lucrative investment, generating significantly higher income than single-let properties. for example, converting a three-bedroom house into a five or six-bedroom multi-let can yield a much higher return. To finance HMOs, obtaining an 80 or 85% loan-to-value mortgage from lenders like Kent Reliance. HMOs are usually renovated to a commercial standard, often with ensuite facilities, making it difficult to revert the property to a single let. Commercial valuations, based on the rental income rather than just the property value, are often sought from banks like Shawbrook Bank. The demand for rooms in the country is high, and you can also explore the rent-to-rent model with HMOs. HMOs offer long-term asset wealth creation and are a great source of passive income, with potential profits ranging from one thousand pounds to two thousand pounds per month. Converting a property into an HMO can take around 12 weeks to complete. HMOs are popular among investors and can be scaled up once you have established the necessary systems and processes.

There are various tenant types to consider, such as local housing authority, students, postgraduates, blue-collar, white-collar, and executive business owners. It is essential to carefully consider tenant mix, which will be discussed further in the planning phase. Throughout the training, we will showcase deals done by personal graduates like Chris, who transitioned from a corporate career to property investment. Chris initially had doubts but decided to take the plunge and seek mentorship. Despite concerns about time and money, he completed his first HMO deal and experienced a positive shift in his life. His success story is just one example of how HMOs can be a game-changer in achieving financial freedom.

Chris initially doubted investing in property due to his lack of experience, and he kept making excuses. As his friend, we encouraged him to take action and try his hand at property investment. We told him he had nothing to lose and needed a mentor to guide him. Chris agreed and paid our mentoring fee, even though we were willing to mentor him for free because he knew that people value what they pay for.

Chris followed the "No Money Down" blueprint and secured funding from investors for his first HMO deal in Felixstowe. The property cost two hundred & thirty-two thousand pounds and required a significant refurbishment of eighty thousand pounds, which his joint venture partner funded. Chris converted the property into eight bedrooms with an average room rate of five hundred & twelve pounds, generating an annual income of forty-nine thousand two hundred pounds. He obtained commercial valuation from Shawbrook Bank, securing a loan to value mortgage of 75%, which enabled him to refinance the property for two hundred and ninety-five thousand pounds.

Although Chris left sixteen thousand five hundred pounds in the deal on the initial refinance, he could recover all of his investment within 8.25 months. After accounting for the mortgage, bills, and maintenance expenses, he generated a monthly profit of two thousand & ten pounds, which equated to sixteen thousand pounds over 8.5 months.

Chris did not take any rental income for the first eight months as agreed with the investor, who received 100% of the profits. Following this period, Chris began taking a split of the rental income after applying sourcing and project management fees and a management fee. Chris was delighted with the success of his first HMO deal, which allowed him to become a full-time property investor, exploring strategies like land development.

HMOs can be a powerful wealth-creation tool for those starting their property investment journey. With the proper guidance and strategy, you can achieve financial freedom and never have to worry about money again.

Land Developments

We understand that you may feel overwhelmed with all the information and strategies in the property portfolio matrix. However, as we guide you through the information provided, you will conclude what is best for you.

Let's delve into land developments, a type of deal we're particularly fond of. The beauty of it is, you don't have to be a seasoned builder, architect, engineer, or a spreadsheet whiz to get involved. Our journey in land development began in 2015, and we didn't have any prior experience as developers. This just goes to show that anyone can venture into this lucrative field.

Land development is a strategic path to long-term wealth creation. It involves acquiring land, with or without planning permission, and constructing commercial or residential units. These units can be rented out, sold, or a combination of both. This strategy not only generates passive income through build-to-rent units but also offers higher profit margins. You have the flexibility to build single lets, HMOs, serviced accommodation, or a combination of these options within one deal, providing a diverse and secure investment portfolio.

It's important to note that land development deals may take some time to complete, often around a year and a half or more. However, the payoff is usually worth the wait. These deals typically involve multiple units, which can significantly boost your property portfolio. for instance, our first land development deal was a prime example. It comprised nine units, seven flats, and two houses at Priory Street Colchester. The entire process took a year to complete, and we were able to sell all units within six months, as it was our JV partners' preferred choice.

Land development is a gateway to expanding your property portfolio and creating additional houses or flats. Allow us to share the details of our first-ever land development deal, a project that left an indelible mark on us. In the images, you can witness the construction process, from demolishing an old yard to piling and the final product. We even had some fun with charity calendar shoots. With the funds raised, we were able to build a home for a deprived family in Popayan, Colombia - a project close to our hearts and a testament to the potential for success in land development.

The beauty of land development deals lies in the fact that the only thing that can hold you back is yourself. However, we strongly advise seeking assistance, support, and accountability, especially for your first land development deal, as it can be a valuable learning experience. This is where the academy can be a game-changer, offering you the opportunity to partner with us for guidance and personal growth.

Let's delve into the details of this specific land development deal. Our objective was to construct nine dwellings, including seven flats and two houses. We acquired the land with planning permission for a total of three hundred and ten thousand pounds, and the estimated construction costs amounted to £1.1 million. The interest we repaid during the process was approximately eighty-six thousand pounds, resulting in a total expenditure of £1.5 million. The projected Gross Development Value (GDV) was £2 million. The potential profit from deals like this could range from around five hundred thousand pounds. In our case, we opted to sell all of the units, as per the preference of one of our investors. However, you have the flexibility to refinance or sell based on your strategy.

Envision the possibility of earning a profit of £250,000 from just one land deal within a year. That's over £20,000 per month, potentially surpassing your current earnings. The world of land development is full of opportunities. Many of our Academy graduates allocate 80% of their spare time to their primary strategy, such as rent-to-rent, while dedicating 20% to secondary strategies like land development or commercial conversions. Previously, we worked with Kevin D'Souza, one of our Academy graduates, on a project. We constructed 14 flats in a vacant space in Loughton, with a GDV around £6 million. It's a testament to the potential success in this field. Here are some pictures of the development:

M&S
MAEDA

5

The aim is to complete at least one land development deal per year in addition to your current endeavours. What's even more exciting is the potential to use the profits from your land deal to further enhance your property portfolio or diversify into other asset classes. This strategy allows you to not only benefit from the immediate returns of land development but also to secure your financial future through smart investment decisions.

Commercial Conversions

So, we've just discussed land development deals. Now, let's have a look at commercial conversions. This is a golden ticket for investors. A commercial unit is anything that is not residential; the conversion of commercial buildings into residential flats requires something called permitted development and prior approval, which was introduced in 2015. This was a golden ticket for all developers. It meant that there were certain types of commercial conversions that you no longer need to apply for planning permission. We will now go through all the regulations and the planning and what you can and cannot do for all of the strategies; you can, like land development, convert to rent, or you can convert to sell (big profits, excellent margins). You want to ensure you make a minimum of 25% on GDV. GDV stands for Gross Development Value, the value of your units once you've done all the building work, the refurb work or the commercial conversion work. So, for example, if you had ten flats, and they were valued at one hundred thousand pounds each, your GDV would be one million pounds. And if you're working on a 25% profit margin, you will want to ensure that at least two hundred & fifty thousand pounds is your profit. This is one of our commercial conversions. We love this deal. We converted two offices into sixteen one-bedroom boutiques, very high-standard apartments. Fifteen sold off plan, and the smallest one sold as soon as we had the show flat ready. It was a superb deal! This is what's great about partnerships and people knowing what you're doing. We called a good friend named Mark and said, 'Hey, Mark, just a little bit of a catch-up. How are you getting on?'

Interestingly, Mark, an experienced developer, informed us that he was doing exceptionally well. He mentioned that they had recently encountered a predicament where an investor had backed out just as they were about to finalise a deal. We couldn't believe the coincidence when we shared that we had an investor available and had unfortunately just experienced a deal falling through. At that moment, we proposed joining forces and collaborating on the project. We combined their existing deal with our investor's funds, forming a formidable partnership. By sharing the workload, we achieved success and had a lot of fun along the way. Surprisingly, it only required a little of our time, as we were rarely on-site, except for capturing a few videos and attending occasional progress meetings. The outcome was rewarding for everyone involved.

Goldmine Areas

This section will focus on selecting the right strategy and identifying your goldmine area. By avoiding the scattergun approach and following our specific criteria, you can feel confident in your investment decisions. This approach prevents you from being pulled in multiple directions and facing varying costs for construction and refurbishment in different areas, ensuring a more secure and profitable investment.

You should invest within one hour of where you live. Look for areas with high rental demand, close to bustling town centres or regions populated with at least eighty thousand residents within a twenty-mile radius of a large town or city. It's also beneficial to have robust transportation links and at least twenty medium to large employers nearby.

Consider a macro location, a generalised area, within a thirty to sixty-minute distance from where you live. for example, if you live in Chelmsford, consider investing in Colchester, as it offers excellent property deals and higher yields and is only twenty minutes down the road with several other smaller towns and villages nearby. Ipswich is also a great hotspot in which to invest.

Investing locally, within an hour of your location, offers significant advantages. It minimizes travel time and the challenging task of building a team in distant areas. Instead, you can focus on finding your micro-location within your chosen area, which could be specific streets or areas with strong market demand. for instance, in Colchester, some areas consistently offer lucrative investment opportunities.

By following specific criteria and choosing the right macro and micro locations, you can find your goldmine area and invest successfully.

If we could secure a property for 50% below market value, we would likely pass on the opportunity if it's not an area where we plan to invest in shortly. When scouting for potential investment locations, we have specific criteria to consider.

We typically look for a corner shop or supermarket within proximity, entertainment options like a bowling alley or cinema within a few miles, easy access to transportation within a ten to twenty-minute walk, and nearby healthcare facilities, including a doctor's office and a significant hospital within a fifteen-minute drive. for properties intended for HMOs (Houses of Multiple Occupancy), we prefer areas without Article 4 restrictions that limit the number of HMOs allowed. Certain regions like Nottingham have Article 4 restrictions, while places like Portsmouth are more HMO-friendly. In contrast, locations like Colchester have no Article 4 restrictions and welcome HMOs, aligning with our investment strategy.

Having a specialised niche area is a game-changer. It simplifies the deal-finding process, boosts the value and returns on investments, saves time, reduces risks, and enhances understanding of financial figures such as conversion costs, new build costs, refurbishment costs, selling prices, and rental prices. Building relationships with local agents adds credibility with investors, deepens local market knowledge, and boosts overall confidence.

Identifying one or two Goldmine areas where growth and expansion opportunities exist is not just advisable, it's a potential pathway to significant success. Especially if your goal is to build a property portfolio, this strategy can inspire and motivate you to achieve tremendous success and scale your property ventures further.
During the initial one to twelve months, when challenges are likely to arise, seeking guidance and support becomes crucial. Joining a resourceful platform like the Assets for Life Academy can provide valuable assistance and knowledge. If you're not already a member, consider joining to access resources and guidance that can significantly assist you in navigating the early stages of your property investment journey.

When considering your local area, thorough research is key. Dive into the housing market and analyze the rental market. Reach out to agents and schedule multiple property viewings to gain a comprehensive understanding of what's working and what's not.

Additionally, explore websites like SpareRoom.com, Airbnb, and Booking.com to understand the rental landscape. Assess whether your area exhibits strong capital growth, higher yields with limited capital growth, or a mixture of both. We will piece together the puzzle as we progress through the remaining chapters and provide further guidance.

We hope you find this information helpful. You must conduct in-depth research on your chosen Goldmine area. Within a thirty to sixty-minute radius of your location, there is a real hotspot for the investment strategy you wish to pursue. To begin, mark your exact location on a map and draw a circle with an hour's drive in all directions. This will help you identify properties closer to you. It is essential to only have properties an hour apart, as it would require a two-hour round trip. Aim to be approximately an hour away from your multiple properties to facilitate managing and building a cluster of profitable property deals in the area.

Where To Find Deals

Now, we will explore where to find incredible property deals, so let's discuss the best strategies for finding them.

Finding deals should be your top priority—obsess over it. Success starts with the right deal, so set weekly targets for viewings and analysis. Even with a busy life, schedule viewings on weekends or evenings. No excuses—maximise your time and push hard.

As you search for deals and make viewings, remember the 80/20 principle. Focus on the efforts that yield the most results. Play smart when making offers, and block out specific times in your diary for viewings. But remember, building trust and rapport with agents is not just a strategy; it's a necessity. You can't expect to walk into an agency for the first time and receive the best deals. You must work hard to earn their respect and trust. This relationship can be the key to unlocking exclusive deals and insider information, so it's worth investing your time and effort.

To find property deals, set up alerts on platforms like Rightmove, Zoopla, and Prime Locations. Use tools like Plot Finder, Land Insights, and the Planning Portal for targeted searches. Contact vendors directly via SpareRoom, OpenRent, or Gumtree, and consider sending letters or distributing leaflets. Explore HMO license lists, auctions, and make phone calls to uncover opportunities.

Remember, persistence is the key to success in this business. Keep searching, keep making connections, and keep exploring various channels. This unwavering commitment will significantly increase your chances of finding exceptional property deals. Please don't get discouraged by the challenges; use them as stepping s tones to your success.

In addition to the mentioned resources, remember to explore Facebook groups and professional platforms like LinkedIn & Skool. Deals can be found everywhere, and it's like deep-sea fishing. If you go out with a small net, you'll catch only a few fish. But if you go out with a big net, your chances of finding more deals increase. So, casting a wide net when searching for deals is crucial.

In our experience, most of our deals come from agents. Therefore, we have invested time in building solid relationships with them. Please explore these portals yourself, but remember this little tip: register with a separate email address dedicated solely to deal alerts and notifications. This will help you manage the influx of information effectively.

Closing your first deal can be tough, but success often leads to more deals. Droughts are normal, so stay persistent and monitor your pipeline. Keep in touch with agents and vendors—about one in three fallen-through deals return, often with motivated sellers, creating great opportunities.

Resources to find deals & land

rightmove PlanningPortal ESTATES GAZETTE

SpareRoom ukland directory LTD tepilo

nimbus PROPERTY SNAKE

Next Steps

As mentioned, finding properties is extensive and has many components to consider. It's important to recap and ensure we cover all the essential aspects before moving on to the next steps.

Firstly, different property strategies are available, and you need to determine which suits you best. Focusing on two strategies simultaneously is recommended, dedicating 80% of your time to your primary strategy and 20% to your secondary one. Additionally, you need to identify the types of agents you should approach. These include land agents, commercial agents, estate agents, and letting agents. Now, let's go over some next steps.

Search Google for local agents in your Goldmine area—land, commercial, letting, and residential. Set up alerts, compile details (names, websites, contacts) in a spreadsheet, and build relationships with at least ten agents in your area.

Next, practice your pitch. Be clear about who you are, what you offer, and what you seek. This will help you when making your approach to the agents.

Once prepared, allocate a morning or a day to visit your Goldmine area. Dress professionally, according to your standards, and drive to the area. Walk into each agent's office, introduce yourself, and establish a connection. Arrange multiple viewings and focus on building trust and credibility with these agents.

Taking these steps will help you progress in your property search journey.

Building a relationship with agents is crucial, and establishing trust and credibility takes some time and effort. When you first approach agents, they might not be receptive but don't give up. Keep making yourself known and following them up. You can do this by making weekly phone calls and showing genuine interest in their listings and work.

You must let them know what differentiates you from other property investors when pitching. Highlight any cash or access to high-net-worth investors that you have.

Persistence is key. You only need a few agents to like and trust you, and they will start bringing you the best deals in the marketplace. If the agent calls you for a viewing, drop everything and go on that viewing to build a relationship.

Initially, you may need to attend viewings of properties you know you won't purchase to build a relationship with the agent. Make the most of the time by having a coffee and getting to know them. Building rapport and making connections can lead to long-term relationships and deals in the future. Remember to share your vision with them and see if you have common interests. This way, you can connect with agents and make deals happen.

If you need help driving to the goldmine area, there's another way to contact agents. Start by listing all the agents in your local area, and aim to call two agents daily, Monday through Friday. Within two weeks, you will have touched base with all the agents on your list.

Don't feel overwhelmed by the thought of calling so many agents. You can fit in the calls during your lunch break and take it slow. Stephen Yates, one of my graduates, initially felt overwhelmed by the number of agents he had to call but made two to three calls daily. Through this process, he established a relationship with agents and even secured his first of many deals.

Remember, the goal is building relationships with agents; every call counts. Take your time, make the calls, and you'll start seeing results.

Introducing Yourself To Agents

Let us take you through another powerful bit of information on effectively introducing yourself to the relevant agent. Here are some key points to keep in mind:

1. **Be prepared:** Ensure that your website is up-to-date, you have a business card, and you have a clear understanding of your branding. It's essential to present yourself professionally.

2. **Be genuine:** Be yourself and be authentic in your approach. Agents appreciate honesty and sincerity.

3. **Know your message:** Clearly understand what you want to convey about your business. for example, if you're approaching estate, land, or commercial agents, mention that you are a property investor from Assets for Life. Discuss the types of properties or projects you focus on, such as buying and selling refurbished houses, building blocks of flats or homes, or commercial conversions.

4. **Find common ground:** Look for shared interests or connections with the agent. This helps to establish rapport and build a stronger relationship.

5. **Highlight high-net-worth investor funds:** Emphasise that you have access to high-net-worth investor funds, which can be an attractive proposition for agents.

6. **Mention recommendations:** You were recommended by someone known to you and the agent. for example, you can say, "I've heard great things about you from another developer named Dave. It's clear that you come highly recommended."

By following these guidelines, you can make a strong and compelling introduction to agents, helping you to establish a productive relationship with them.

'I just wanted to pop in and introduce myself, see what properties you have available, and express our ability to move quickly.' By presenting yourself confidently, discussing the specific property types you're interested in, and mentioning your access to high-net-worth investor funds, you'll capture the agents' interest as a property investor. Remember to approach them confidently, as if you're talking to a friend, as we're all on the same level playing field here.

When dealing with letting agents or calling for rent-to-rent deals, it's essential to use the right approach. Avoid mentioning "rent to rent" or "guaranteed rent," ensure you have your website and business cards ready. Registering with the Property Ombudsman will position you as an equal within the same governing body. Introduce yourself as a relocation company, such as "Hey John, my name is Liam, and my company is Assets for Life UK -

Building solid relationships with letting agents is crucial. Let them know what type of property and area you're interested in and ask if they have any suitable rentals available. There are a few essential questions to ask the letting agent, including:

1. Is the two-bedroom property on Hastings Road still available?
2. Is the landlord open to a long-term tenant? We're looking for an initial 12-month term with the option to extend.
3. Would the landlord consider a company let?

Always be prepared to address objections and overcome challenges. Mention that your company is registered with the ombudsman and that you work with professionals from various industries nationwide. Remember, it's not always brain surgeons; you also work with individuals in construction, aviation, and the medical field.

Expect rejection and objections when approaching agents, but don't let it discourage you. Keep your confidence high, a nd remember to earn their trust and respect over time.

We hope you found these tips helpful. It's essential to position yourself correctly, make confident phone calls, and approach agents with a positive mindset.

In our journey through site findings, it's essential to highlight the inspiring story of Andrew Gray, whose success is a testament to the power of strategic site selection and meticulous planning. Andrew's journey began with a single Buy-to-Let property, but his vision and determination propelled him to transform a three-bedroom semi-detached house into a high-end seven-bedroom HMO. This ambitious project, fraught with challenges, underscored the importance of choosing the right site and understanding the local market dynamics. Andrew's ability to navigate these complexities and deliver a profitable, high-quality development exemplifies the potential that lies in careful site selection and thorough market analysis. To delve deeper into Andrew's remarkable achievements and learn more about his journey, be sure to check out the final chapter of this book.

In conclusion, your property investment success begins with the knowledge and strategies you've gained. By researching postcodes and using the Portfolio Matrix, you can unlock high-potential areas and reduce risks. Each strategy, from rent-to-rent to land developments, offers a path toward financial freedom.

Stay focused on your goals, build strong relationships, and leverage funding and partnerships. With persistence and strategic planning, you'll create a diversified property portfolio. Embrace challenges, adapt to the market, and pursue your dreams to build wealth and a lasting legacy. The opportunities are yours—seize them and succeed.

Assignment

1. **Conduct a Site Analysis:**
   Choose a target area or postcode, research factors like employment, schools, amenities, transport, and market conditions, then create a report assessing the site's investment potential.

2. **Identify Your Primary and Secondary Strategies:**
   Review the Portfolio Matrix and choose two property strategies that align with your goals and resources. Briefly explain why you selected these strategies and how they fit into your overall investment plan.

3 **Set Up Alerts and Find Deals:**
Register on property platforms such as Rightmove, Zoopla, and other relevant websites. Set up alerts for your chosen strategies and start identifying potential deals. List five properties that match your criteria and explain why they are good investment opportunities.

4 **Prepare Your Pitch:**
Develop a pitch to introduce yourself to property agents. Include your investment goals, the types of properties you are interested in, and any funding or investor backing you have. Practice delivering this pitch confidently.

5 **Network with Agents:**
Compile a list of at least ten property agents in your goldmine area. Plan visits to their offices or make phone calls to introduce yourself and establish relationships. Document your interactions and any potential leads or deals that arise from these connections.

6 **Evaluate Potential Deals:**
For each property you identify, perform a preliminary analysis. Calculate potential rental income, refurbishment costs, and expected profits. Determine whether each deal aligns with your investment strategy and goals.

7 **Create a Portfolio Plan:**
Outline a plan for building your property portfolio over the next year. Include your primary and secondary strategies, target areas, funding plans, and expected milestones. Set specific, measurable goals for the number of deals you aim to secure and the income you hope to generate.

This assignment will help you apply the concepts from Chapter 3, ensuring you are well-prepared to identify, evaluate, and secure profitable property deals in your chosen market. Take this knowledge, turn it into action, and watch your property investment dreams become reality.

READY TO DIVE DEEPER INTO PROPERTY STRATEGIES? VISIT OUR EVENT PAGE TO EXPLORE COMPREHENSIVE TRAINING OPPORTUNITIES, GAIN EXPERT INSIGHTS, AND DISCOVER THE PATH TO BUILDING YOUR SUCCESSFUL PORTFOLIO!

CHAPTER FOUR

APPRAISAL

An essential aspect of property investment is appraisal, which involves assessing the value of a property. A property appraisal is a detailed evaluation conducted by a professional appraiser to determine the fair market value of a property. This valuation process considers the property's location, size, condition, comparable sales in the area, and current market trends. Appraisals are crucial for buyers and sellers as they help ensure the property is priced accurately and reasonably. Additionally, lenders rely on property appraisals to determine the amount of financing they can provide for a property, and this is where the severe figures come in. A thorough understanding of property appraisal is vital for making informed decisions in real estate transactions and maximising your investment potential.

Property appraisals provide critical information that can affect property transactions and investment decisions. The appraisal process determines the property's actual market value and helps to identify factors that may impact the property's value. for investors, appraisals can provide valuable information to identify potential investment opportunities and help ensure that properties are correctly valued. Understanding the appraisal process not only empowers property owners to appeal property tax assessments, negotiate rental rates, and evaluate the profitability of an investment property, but also gives them a sense of control and confidence in their real estate decisions. Overall, property appraisal is a crucial aspect of property investment that can have far-reaching implications and should be taken seriously by anyone involved in property transactions.

So, welcome to the Numbers section of dealing with properties. In this module, we will dive into the financial aspects of property investment, including analysing deals, calculating costs, and ensuring profitability. By understanding the numbers side of property investing, you'll have the knowledge and skills to make informed decisions and maximise your return on investment. This chapter will explore key metrics, general costs, and essential numbers integral to property investment. We will also examine how these factors can vary depending on the specific property strategy you choose to employ. Understanding these differences will give you valuable insights to navigate various property investment scenarios effectively. This understanding is not just beneficial, it's crucial for your success in property investment. Let's delve into these fundamental aspects, empowering you to make informed decisions and thrive in the exciting world of property investment.

Rental yield is calculated by dividing annual net rental income by the property value. For example, £20,000 net income on a £200,000 property gives a 10% yield. However, to assess profitability more fully, we use metrics like return on capital employed (ROCE) and return on investment (ROI), which account for all costs, including legal and agent fees. ROI is calculated by dividing net rental income by the total purchase price plus expenses. For instance, £12,000 income on a £250,000 investment gives a 4.8% ROI, offering a more complete picture of investment profitability.

Another important metric for us is the return on capital employed. This metric is more significant for us than the net rental income. It is calculated by dividing the net rental income by the capital invested, which is the money you contribute from your pocket. In this scenario, we assume that a bank or another party finances most of the purchase price, so the capital invested refers only to the deposit. for example, if the net rental income is twelve thousand pounds and the capital invested is seventy-five thousand pounds, the return on capital employed would be 16%.

Refinancing (BRR) allows you to retrieve your initial investment. The return on capital left in the deal is calculated by dividing net rental income by the money remaining after refinancing. For example, £12,000 income with £20,000 left in the deal gives a 60% return. Our target is infinite return, meaning no money left in the deal. For instance, our Colchester project achieved an infinite return, covering all costs and generating £6,000 profit. This potential for high returns should inspire your property investment journey:

Single let: Minimum net profit of £300 per month

Flip: £30,000 profit

High cash-flowing deal (Rent-to-Rent or HMO): £15,000 profit per year per property

Land Development or Commercial Conversion: £250,000 profit.

Moving on, let's discuss some general costs you need to know. We will delve into these costs in more detail in the DNA analysis section, but for now, we will provide you with some ballpark figures. Here are the essential costs you should consider:

1. **Purchase price:** This is the cost of acquiring the property.
2. **Stamp duty:** You need to factor in the stamp duty tax payable on the property.
3. **Legal costs** are the fees associated with hiring a solicitor or conveyancer.
4. **Refurbishment cost:** Consider the expenses involved in renovating or improving the property.
5. **Costs of borrowing:** If you are financing the purchase through a loan or mortgage, keep interest payments in mind.
6. **JV (Joint Venture) finance:** If you are partnering with someone for financing, consider any associated costs or profit-sharing arrangements.
7. **Council tax during refurbishment:** Determine whether you need to cover the council tax payments while renovating the property.
8. **Development insurance:** You may also need insurance coverage during the development phase and afterwards.
9. **Accounting:** It is recommended to operate through a limited company to take advantage of tax offsets, so accounting fees should be considered.
10. **Management fees:** If you plan to hire a property management company, factor in their costs.

11. **Internet costs:** Once the property is up and running, you may need to pay for internet services.
12. **Repair and maintenance:** Allocate a budget for repairing any damages or regular maintenance.
13. **Void periods:** Depending on the area, you may experience periods where the property is unoccupied.

Allocate a percentage of the rental income to cover these potential voids.

Ensure you consider these costs when analysing your potential investment to understand the overall financial implications better.

General Numbers You Need To Know

Cost to Build:
This refers to the total expenditure required to construct a building or structure on the property. It includes labour, materials, permits, and other construction-related expenses. for an accurate estimate, obtaining quotes from builders or contractors is advisable.

Refurbishment Cost:
If the property already has an existing structure, this cost represents the amount needed for renovation or refurbishment. It may include repainting, installing new fixtures, or significant overhauls like plumbing or electrical work. It's recommended to consult a reputable contractor to obtain a precise estimate.

Purchase Price:
This is the amount paid to acquire the property and depends on location, condition, size, and current real estate market conditions.

Profit:
Profit is the net income generated from the property deal after deducting all expenses (including purchase, construction or refurbishment, and associated costs) from the sale price or rental income.

Closing Costs:
These are fees and expenses incurred beyond the property's purchase price during the transfer of ownership from the seller to the buyer. They may include attorney fees, title insurance, appraisal fees, and more.

Holding Costs:
These are the expenses incurred while owning the property before it is sold or rented out. They may include mortgage payments, property taxes, insurance, and maintenance costs.

Accurately estimating these costs is essential before engaging in a property deal to ensure profitability. It is generally advisable to overestimate costs and underestimate returns to mitigate unexpected expenses or market fluctuations.

In Chapter 4, Appraisal, we delve into the critical aspects of property valuation and financial metrics, essential for making informed investment decisions. A shining example of mastering these principles is Oliver Roworth, whose journey from a chartered structural engineer to a successful property developer is truly inspiring. Oliver's meticulous approach to appraising properties and understanding financial metrics has enabled him to secure his first land development deal with a potential Gross Development Value (GDV) of £1.25 million. His ability to navigate the complexities of property appraisal and leverage his engineering background has been instrumental in his success. To learn more about Oliver's remarkable achievements and his detailed approach to property appraisal, be sure to check out the final chapter of this book.

Mastering property appraisal and understanding financial metrics is the backbone of successful property investment. With the knowledge you've gained in this chapter, you're now equipped to assess property values accurately, analyse deals, and make informed decisions that maximise your investment returns. Embrace these concepts and let them guide your investment journey.

Remember, the true power of property investment lies in understanding and controlling the numbers. From calculating rental yields and return on investment to leveraging financing options and minimising costs, your ability to navigate these financial waters will set you apart from the average investor. This knowledge will empower you to seize lucrative opportunities and build a robust and diversified portfolio that withstands market fluctuations.

The road ahead is filled with opportunities for those who are prepared. Stay diligent, refine your skills, and approach each investment confidently and precisely. Your dedication to mastering these financial principles will pave the way for long-term success and economic freedom. The world of property investment is yours to conquer—go out there, apply these strategies, and watch your property empire grow!

Assignment

1. **Conduct a Property Appraisal:**
Choose a property you are interested in and conduct a detailed appraisal. for instance, consider a property in [specific location], with a size of [specific square footage], in [specific condition]. Research comparable sales in the area, such as [sold property prices], and current market trends, like [specific market trends], then write a comprehensive report summarizing your findings and providing an estimated market value for the property, such as [specific estimated market value].

2. **Calculate Rental Yield:**
Please select a property and calculate its rental yield. Determine the annual net rental income (after deducting expenses) and divide it by the property's value. Write down your calculations and explain what the rental yield indicates about the investment's potential.

3. **Analyse Return on Investment (ROI) and Return on Capital employed:**
Calculate the ROI and the return on capital employed using the property from the previous steps. Include all associated costs, such as purchase price, legal fees, and refurbishment costs. Explain how these metrics help you understand the profitability of the investment.

4. **Create a Cost Breakdown:**
List all potential costs involved in property investment, including purchase price, stamp duty, legal fees, refurbishment costs, borrowing costs, JV finance, council tax during refurbishment, development insurance, accounting fees, management fees, internet costs, repair and maintenance, and void periods. Provide estimated figures for each cost and explain how they impact the overall investment analysis.

5. **Evaluate a Deal Using BRR Strategy:**
Find a property that could be suitable for the Buy, Refurbish, Refinance (BRR) strategy. Calculate the potential return on capital left in the deal after refinancing. Use a hypothetical scenario if necessary and outline the steps involved in the process.

6. **Set Financial Goals and Targets:**
Based on the strategies and metrics discussed in this chapter, set specific financial goals for your property investments. Determine your target net profit for different deals (e.g., single lets, flips, high cash-flowing deals, land development). Write down these goals and explain how you plan to achieve them.

This assignment will solidify your understanding of property appraisal and financial metrics, ensuring you are well-prepared to make intelligent and profitable investment decisions. Take these lessons to heart, apply them in real estate endeavours, and watch your property portfolio thrive.

CHAPTER FIVE

PLANNING

Step five is planning, another favourite step of ours. Planning is all about building your Power Team. Planning is about knowing the rules and regulations for the matrix's different types of property strategies. What can you do? What can't you do? You should be building a professional property business. It would help if you were not cutting corners; you must do things legally. Planning is also about planning your time and planning your team. What can you do to be the most efficient property owner as a business owner? You want to focus on the right tasks. You want to focus on areas in your business where you can bring in the most money in the shortest time. So planning is essential.

Planning is Key in Property Development

When purchasing a site, remember that the Gross Development Value (GDV) is heavily determined by the planning permission you secure. The letter from the console permitting you to build is crucial—it's what the specific development you're planning, such as a residential or commercial project, is all about. Funders will ask you immediately: do you have planning permission for these developments? This can make or break the funding process. Many assume they'll quickly get planning permission, but it's a risky gamble. Pay close attention to this section, as planning permission is a critical step that you cannot overlook.

Before delving further into planning, take a moment to assess your own value. Consider how much you are currently earning per hour in your job. In property development, income-generating activities could include finding undervalued properties, negotiating favourable deals, managing properties for a fee, or even renting out properties for a steady income. Focus on these activities and delegate tasks that can be outsourced to others. The key is to focus on activities that directly contribute to your income and the growth of your property portfolio.

While some may stress the importance of money, we believe that deals are the key to success in property development. Discovering a great deal can open doors to flexibility—if funding is challenging, you can still potentially profit from selling the deal to someone else. Money is undoubtedly important, but deals are the foundation of success in this field, offering a world of possibilities and potential benefits.

Remember, property development revolves around the interplay of money and deals. Focus on honing your skills in both aspects to maximise your success in the industry. Keep this in mind as you navigate the intricate world of property development.

Your vision should be the heart of your company, guiding your every move. It defines your current position and your future aspirations. The act of writing down your vivid vision is of utmost importance. At AFL, we create a three-year vision that explicitly outlines our goals. for now, concentrate on the 'what' and the 'how' will follow. Ensuring that you document your vision is a key step towards maintaining focus and determination in your property development journey.

Surrounding your vision, you'll find other elements. First, consider your property goals—how many properties do you wish to manage, build, or sell? Next, think about your financial strategy. How will you find and secure deals? Will you establish an administrative team to handle property management? Defining the quality of tenants you want to attract and establishing effective marketing strategies is crucial. Be it Facebook campaigns, YouTube channels, or Instagram, develop a plan for each channel. Lastly, embrace the role of technology in your property journey. Consider the technical resources available, such as property management software, virtual reality for property tours, or online platforms for property listings, and leverage them to align with the current demands of the industry, such as conducting online viewings.

By incorporating your vision and addressing these key areas, you can set a solid foundation for your property journey. Remember to update and adapt your vision as your company evolves continuously.

Planning your time:

The world of property entrepreneurship can be a whirlwind of activity. Something always demands your attention, from scouting locations and finding deals to building relationships and raising capital. But the key to success isn't just staying busy—it's staying productive. And that begins with efficient planning. Consider the concept of the "time value of money." In finance, this principle suggests that a dollar today is worth more than a dollar tomorrow. Why? Because time is a limited and valuable resource. Just as you would invest money wisely to get the best return, so should you invest your time.

As a property entrepreneur, your focus should be on high-income-generating tasks. These are activities that directly contribute to your bottom line and growth. Here are some examples:

1. **Building Relationships:** Networking with other entrepreneurs, investors, real estate agents, and contractors can open doors to new opportunities.
2. **Sales and Marketing:** Selling properties and marketing your business is crucial for generating income and attracting new customers.
3. **Raising Money:** Whether seeking out investors or applying for loans, securing funds is critical to keep your operations running and expand your portfolio.
4. **Finding Deals:** Locating undervalued properties or potential development sites can generate substantial profits.

Contrast these activities with low-income-generating tasks like administrative work, inventory management, and minor repairs. While these tasks are necessary, they contribute little to your income and can often be outsourced or delegated.

How, then, can you manage your time more efficiently? Here are some strategies:

Utilise Diary Systems: A well-organized diary can help you schedule your time effectively, ensuring you focus on high-impact tasks. Set aside specific blocks of time for different activities and stick to your schedule.

Limit Time Wasters: Identify and eliminate distractions in your day, this might mean turning off the television, limiting social media usage, or setting boundaries with interruptions.

Make Sacrifices: Successful entrepreneurship often requires sacrifices. You may need to forego leisure activities or personal engagements to focus on your business. Remember, the success of your venture depends on the time and effort you're willing to invest. In conclusion, efficient planning and time management can significantly impact your success as a property entrepreneur. By focusing on high-income tasks and implementing effective strategies, you'll be well on your way to achieving your entrepreneurial goals.

Power team

Building the right team for Property Development is paramount!

Another crucial aspect of property development is assembling the right team. Surrounding yourself with the right individuals is essential as they become an extension of your company. Whether it's an estate agent, architect, or structural engineer, each member of your power team plays a vital role. Therefore, it is imperative to be highly selective when choosing the right people for your project. Here are some key team members to consider:

1. **Planning Consultant:** Having a highly skilled planning consultant is crucial. David Camp, one of the best planners in our family, leads our team. We also have other dedicated consultants who can help with your project.
2. **Broker for Development Funding:** Before you begin construction, having your broker on board is essential. They will assist you in ensuring your construction plans meet the funding requirements. Different brokers specialise in residential, senior funding, or purely commercial projects. We have a recommended broker list available with discounted prices.
3. **Joint Venture Partner:** Depending on your preferences, you may choose a hands-off or hands-on joint venture partner to collaborate with on your projects.

4. **Business Partner:** You may have one or multiple business partners who contribute to the success of your venture.

5. **Architects:** Architects are vital members of your team who specialise in different types of projects. Select them based on their expertise in land developments, commercial-to-residential conversions, or refurbishments. Sometimes, you may hire architectural technicians or CAD specialists to minimise costs.

6. **Builder:** The builder you choose carries the highest risk in your project. It is crucial to be extremely thorough when selecting a builder. We will provide you with a comprehensive module on successfully appointing a builder, so pay close attention.

7. **Solicitor:** A competent solicitor must handle legal matters, especially if you plan on forming a limited company. Make sure to choose a corporate solicitor who understands the specific requirements of your project.

Avoid the mistakes we made at the beginning of our journey by selecting the right team members and ensuring they are competent to fulfil their roles. Building a solid team increases your chances of success in the property development industry.

Understanding Your Customers in Building a Product

When embarking on a building project, one of the first things to consider is your target customers. Whether you are catering to first-time buyers, tenants, or any other specific group, it is crucial to understand your clients deeply. To assist in this understanding, we have developed a series of questions that you should be able to answer accurately and efficiently. By having a solid grasp of your customers' preferences, you can tailor your product to their needs. Here are some key questions to consider:

1. **Customer Demographics:** Understand who your customers are in terms of age, gender, and occupation. This knowledge will help you shape your product to suit their specific requirements.

2. **Lifestyle Preferences:** Identify where your customers work and frequent in their free time. This knowledge will allow you to position your product in a location that attracts them.

3. **Unique Selling Proposition:** Determine what sets your product apart from the competition and why customers should choose you. Highlight the unique benefits or features that make your offering stand out.

4. **Customer Transformation:** Consider how your product can positively impact or enhance your customers' lives. Identify how your product will address their needs or aspirations.

By carefully analysing the answers to these questions, you can reverse-engineer your product to cater to your target customer's preferences. This approach applies whether you are building houses, renting rooms on a serviced accommodation or HMO basis, or even developing single apartments. By understanding your customers, you can design and create a product that meets their desires and expectations.

Understanding Planning Permission

In property entrepreneurship, a grasp of the planning permission process is crucial in the UK. This regulatory step ensures that any construction or alterations adhere to local and national standards. Let's delve into this process and other important rules and regulations involved.

Step 1 - Determine the Need for Planning Permission: Planning permission is the consent required from your Local Planning Authority (LPA) for building new structures or making significant changes to existing buildings. It's important to note that not all development projects necessitate planning permission. Therefore, the first step is to establish whether your project requires it.

Step 2 - Contact Your LPA's Planning Department: If you determine that planning permission is necessary, the following action is to contact your LPA through your local council. They will provide guidance and support throughout the application process. There are a range of specialists available depending on the type of project, and this is one of the benefits of the Assets for Life academy, our clients get access to our range of experts.

Step 3 - Submit an Application: Most applications are completed online through the Planning Portal or the authority's website. The application will entail providing details of your plans, including any potential impact on the local environment and community. We strongly recommend this is carried out by a trusted or recommended planning consultant from a reputable source.

Step 4 - Await the Decision: Once the application is submitted, it goes through various stages, such as validation, consultation, and assessment, before a decision is reached. This process typically takes up to eight weeks for minor applications, while more complex ones can take over 13 weeks.

It is important to note that planning permissions often come with conditions stipulating that development must commence within three years of approval.

Rules & Regulations

In addition to planning permission, some other important rules and regulations must be considered when planning property builds in the UK. One such regulation is building regulations approval, which establishes standards for the design, construction, and alterations of nearly all buildings. These regulations are developed by the UK government and approved by Parliament.

If your property is listed or located in a conservation area, you may also need to apply for listed building or conservation area consent. Before commencing any work, you must check with your Local Planning Authority (LPA) to ensure you have obtained all the necessary permissions. Understanding and navigating the planning permission process and the associated regulations is crucial for property entrepreneurs. By adhering to these regulations, you maintain the integrity of your project and ensure its legality and compliance with local and national standards.

Additionally, knowing other regulations that may apply to your property build is essential. These include fire safety requirements, energy efficiency standards, access and mobility restrictions, and environmental considerations. Adhering to these regulations is not only necessary for legal compliance but also ensures the safety, comfort, and sustainability of the building.

Fire safety regulations include adequate escape routes, fire-resistant materials, smoke detectors, and fire extinguishers. These regulations aim to minimise the risk of fire and ensure the safety of occupants. On the other hand, energy efficiency standards focus on reducing the environmental impact of buildings and improving energy performance. This can include requirements for insulation, heating and cooling systems, lighting efficiency, and renewable energy integration. Compliance with these standards helps reduce carbon emissions and results in long-term cost savings for both the property owner and the occupants. Access and mobility regulations ensure that buildings are accessible to all individuals, including those with disabilities. This can include provisions for wheelchair access, ramps, elevators, and accessible facilities. Creating an inclusive and accessible environment meets legal requirements and reflects a commitment to equality and diversity.

Environmental considerations, such as sustainable materials, waste management practices, and water conservation, play a significant role in modern property development. Adopting environmentally friendly practices can reduce the overall carbon footprint and promote sustainable living.

By staying informed about these regulations and integrating them into your property planning process, you can create a space that meets legal requirements, prioritises safety and accessibility, promotes energy efficiency, and contributes to environmental sustainability. Engaging with experts, such as architects, building contractors, and consultants, can provide valuable guidance and ensure compliance with all relevant regulations throughout the property build .

Landlord checklist

As a landlord, it is essential to start your journey with a robust tenancy agreement in place. This agreement provides legal protection and sets out the terms and responsibilities for you and your tenants. While holiday lets may not require such agreements, for Houses in Multiple Occupation (HMOs), it is crucial to have a well-crafted tenancy agreement.

Additionally, for HMOs, having an inventory list is highly recommended. It is advisable to keep this list as simple as possible by taking pictures and videos of the property's condition. In any dispute or discrepancies,

visual evidence will support your position and help resolve conflicts efficiently.
Utilizing a tenancy deposit scheme is now the norm for landlords. It is vital to send the tenant's deposit to a recognized and authorized scheme such as MyDeposits. This scheme safeguards the deposit and ensures it is handled correctly, providing both parties protection and peace of mind.

Another crucial aspect of being a landlord is obtaining landlord insurance. This insurance provides coverage for damages, liabilities, and other unforeseen circumstances. It is prudent to have adequate insurance for the property itself and its contents, as incidents that might result in financial losses can occur.

Conducting tenant referencing is a significant step in the screening process. A recommended option is to utilize the National Landlords Association (NLA) or another reputable agency to perform credit checks on potential tenants. However, it is advisable to rely on something other than credit checks. Contacting current and previous employers or obtaining character references is wise to gain a more comprehensive understanding of the tenant's background and reliability.

Being thorough will help protect your property investment and ensure a smoother and more secure tenancy. Building a good relationship with reliable tenants is vital for long-term success as a landlord.

Punctuality can indeed speak volumes about a person's character. Assessing the reliability of a potential tenant's employer is an essential factor to consider. Their employment history and stability provide valuable insights into their commitment and ability to fulfil their financial obligations. Consequently, as a landlord, focusing on employment when evaluating potential tenants can be a significant factor in decision-making. Determining an appropriate room rate is crucial for attracting tenants and remaining competitive. Assessing whether you offer better value for money than your competition is essential. Conducting thorough market research and adjusting your room rates will help you stay competitive and attract suitable tenants.

Effective advertising plays a vital role in finding suitable tenants for your property. Exploring various advertising methods, such as online listings or local property portals, is worth exploring. Additionally, having notice boards outside the property can also be beneficial in attracting potential tenants. However, displaying a board may require permission from the relevant authorities, such as your local council or estate agent.

To stay compliant with regulations, it is crucial to have your contact details displayed on the property. This information ensures accessibility for both existing tenants and potential renters. Additionally, including necessary documentation on the boards, such as gas certificates and information about your tenant finding procedure, can help provide transparency and build trust with prospective tenants.

By considering these factors and following proper guidelines, you can effectively market your property, attract reliable tenants, and ensure legal compliance throughout the rental process.

Floorplans

Let's dive into a critical topic - floor plans. In our opinion, the layout is king! It's similar to how cash is king when managing finances.
We want to share a property Jay purchased five years ago when he started his journey. The property is a terraced house located in Colchester. As you can see in the floor plan, there's a little hole at the entrance, followed by a corridor leading to the kitchen and ample living space on the right. Additionally, there's a garage, making it a detached property with two stories. Once you go upstairs, you have four rooms - one decent-sized, two middle-sized, and one that's very small.

As an investor/property owner, we had several options with this property, which we purchased in cash for £250,000. During our analysis process, we meticulously presented the options to our investors. It was crucial to have these options and discuss them in detail to ensure we made the most informed decisions. We explained our options for a six-bedroom HMO, seven-bedroom HMO, or a refurbished HMO that better caters to the needs of our target audience. Additionally, we also explained the associated costs, providing a comprehensive understanding of the potential outcomes.' HMO and the associated costs, providing a comprehensive understanding of the potential outcomes.

Our approach was strategic and meticulous. We identified areas of wasted space, such as the gap on one side and the central aisle. These were not just empty spaces, but opportunities for improvement. We decided to fill these gaps, extend the kitchen, and replace some structural walls to enhance the space's functionality. We designed a clever system to replace one of the structural walls we removed. This was not just a renovation, but a strategic transformation. A well-designed layout can revolutionise a property, and making the most of every inch of space is crucial. Thoroughly discussing options can lead to the best possible outcome for your investment.

We decided to extend the property at the back and create a conservatory while also converting the garage. This allowed us to add one room on the ground floor, making it a self-contained unit with three rooms. In the previous layout, there was only a large living room in that area, but we also made room for a shower.

Upstairs, we made significant changes to maximise the space. The existing rooms were already spacious, but we saw potential for improvement. We created two ensuite bathrooms using some space, and we also made a new wall and created another room. This resulted in four rooms on one side and three on the other. We now had eight bedrooms with the self-contained unit and the converted garage. The transformation was remarkable, and the property's potential was fully realised.

There are a few nuggets of information to take note of. When positioning bathrooms back to back, it's crucial to consider the location of services and drains, especially in a detached property. for easy accessibility, we ensured the drain pipes were directed towards the maintenance hole at the back. This helps save both materials and time during the construction process. Additionally, we built a conservatory as a communal area, providing extra space for the residents.

Now, let's move on to another attractive property. We purchased this one in 2015, one of our first properties in the AFL family. Unlike the previous property, this was a terraced house, and the images depict the front and back of the property.

At the front of the property was initially one small bedroom measuring 6.42 square meters. However, upon inspection, an officer informed us it was too small to be considered habitable as the minimum requirement for a habitable space is 6.5 square meters. We had to make changes to comply with regulations. Additionally, the garage could have been utilised more, so we converted it into a room. There was also a toilet in that area.

Moving on to the upstairs layout, there was a living room, kitchen, and bathroom. On the second floor, there were three bedrooms, which needed to be arranged optimally. We decided to reconfigure the layout.

We connected the existing bathroom and kitchen on the first floor to create one larger space. The previous bathroom was converted into an ensuite for one of the rooms. Additionally, we utilised a wasted space by converting the living room into a spacious bedroom with its own ensuite. This room became one of the largest at 8.2 square meters, generating good cash flow for us.

On the second floor, there was a bathroom and a sink area. We transformed this into two bathrooms, one communal for two rooms and one ensuite for another. The smallest ensuite bathroom measured only 2.02 square meters but was a wide space and brought in consistent rental income.

There was also a challenge with one of the rooms on this floor. The space was initially less than the required 6 .5 square meters, and we had to demolish a wall and move it slightly to create more room. However, we realised we could have made the wardrobe space livable without destroying the entire wall. This was an essential lesson in maximising livable space within the property.

Another obstacle was the wardrobe placement in a corner where it could not be moved due to the height difference. This forced us to relocate it and make adjustments to the room layout.

Ultimately, we not only successfully converted this three-bedroom terraced house into a six-bedroom HMO (House in Multiple Occupation), but we also recouped all our investment and made an additional profit of £6000. This outstanding result translates into an infinite return on investment, a testament to the potential of strategic renovations in the real estate market. This property is a shining example of how careful planning and execution can lead to significant financial gains.

Here are before and after versions of the floor plans:

Ground Floor - *Before*

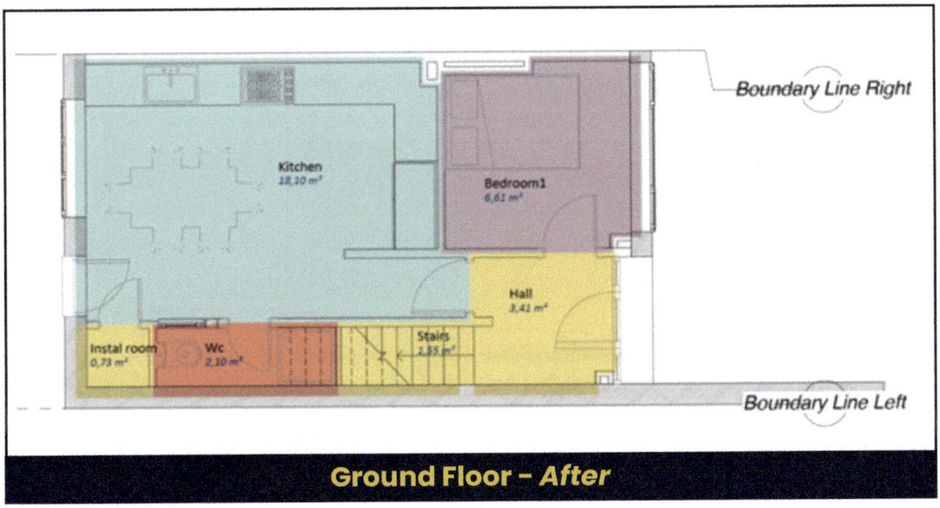

Ground Floor - *After*

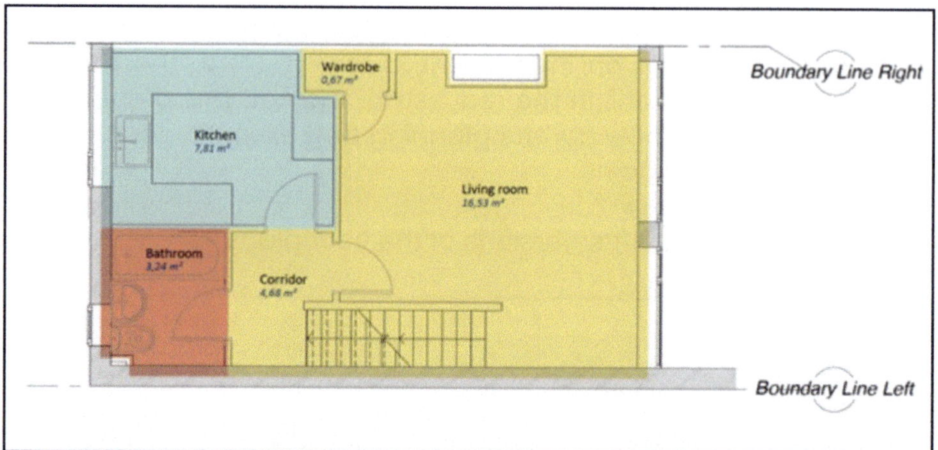

First Floor - *Before*

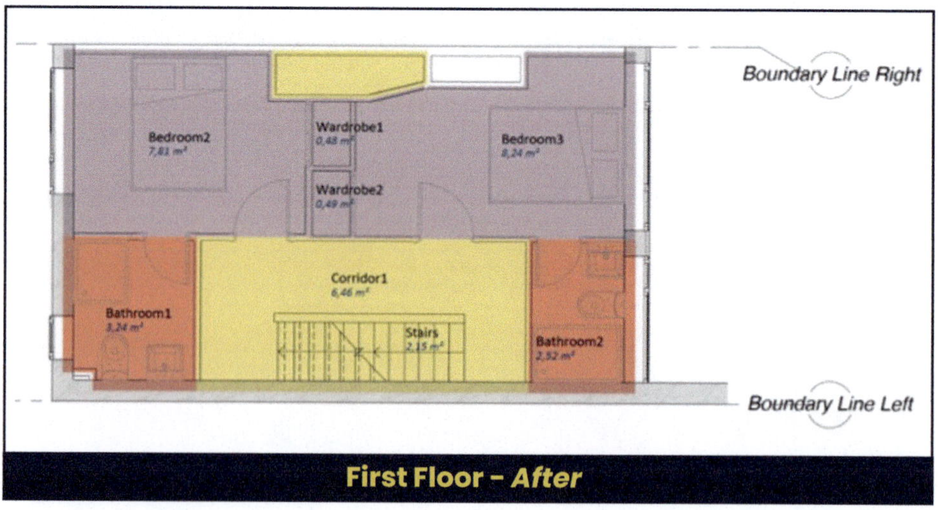

First Floor - *After*

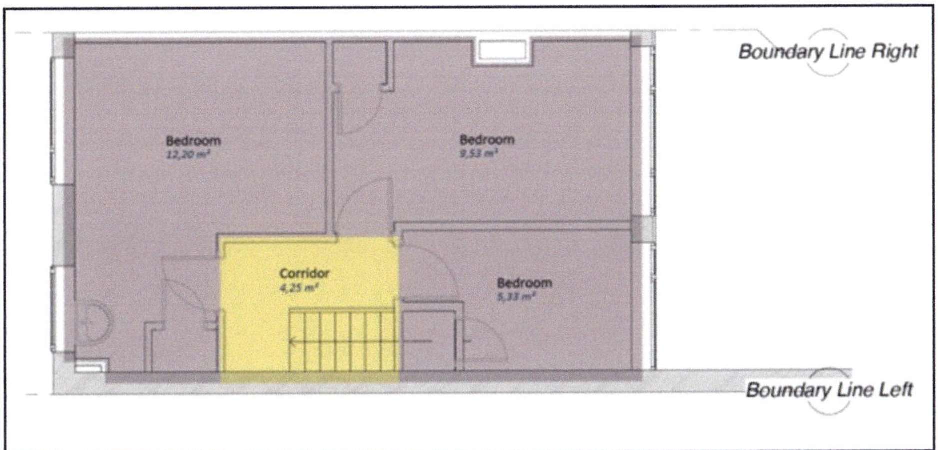

Second Floor - *Before*

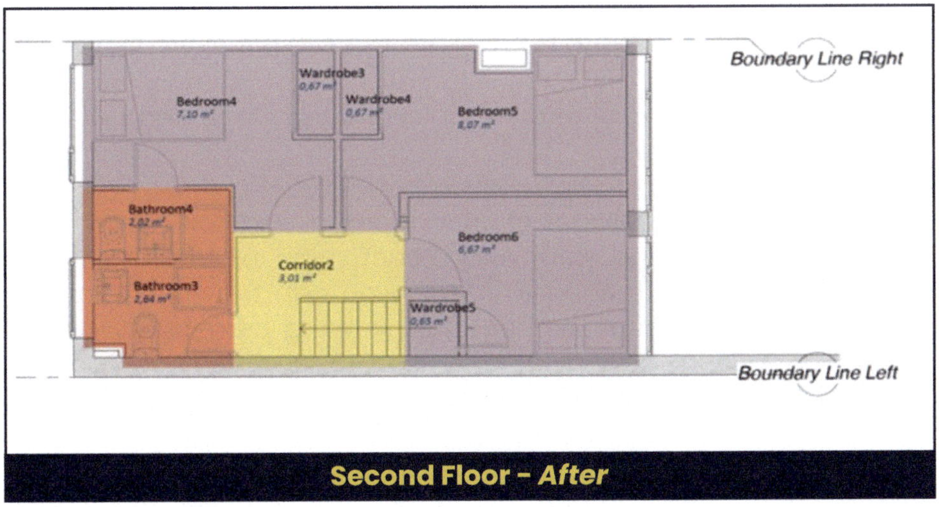

Second Floor - *After*

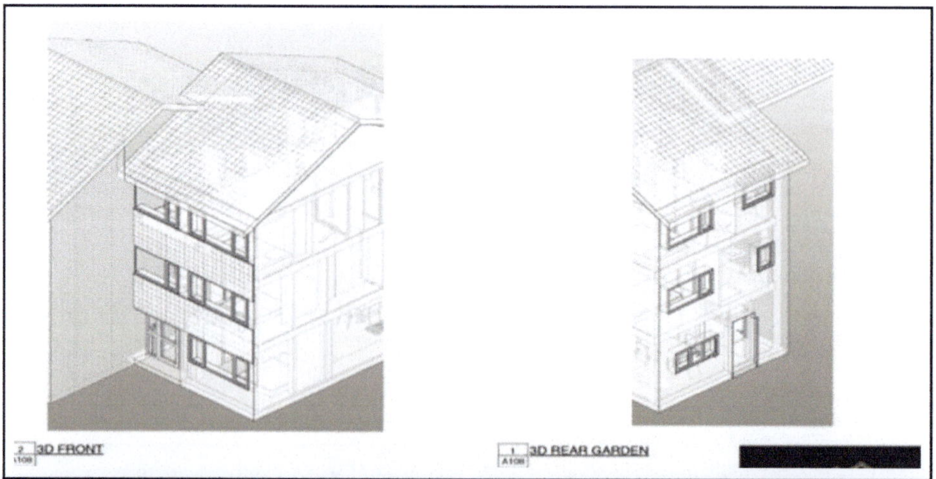

3D Render of the Property

Prior Approval

There are no strict size requirements, but units larger than 30 square meters are preferred by lenders, as smaller units may limit options to cash buyers. If refinancing the whole building, different considerations apply. Prior approval applications cost £80, and for AFL members, we offer discounted rates through experienced planning consultants. Traditional planning applications can cost £350–£1,000 per unit and take up to two years, while prior approval takes just 56 days, offering a faster, more cost-effective alternative.

Therefore, prior approval offers a quicker alternative, and I will also discuss its advantages.

Let's discuss the advantages of prior approval and how it eliminates the need for planning permission. Each type of building has a specific use class attached to it, and you can transition between specific courses without the need for planning permission, making it a straightforward paperwork exercise. Prior approval can only be refused if the building is listed or state-related concerns exist.

Let's go into more detail about using classes to provide more clarity. B1(a) refers to offices, A1 and A2 are for retail purposes, B(e) allows for storage, B1(c) is for light industrial use, and agricultural buildings also fall under permitted development rights for conversion into residential properties. This is fantastic news as it removes the need for planning permission and relieves you of obligations such as section 106 or affordable housing requirements, which can sometimes hinder projects.

Here's an example: when we were considering a conversion a couple of years ago, we had the option of demolition, which incurred additional costs due to a required contribution of over £250,000 for just 16 units. This demonstrates how costs can escalate. However, with permitted development rights, you can save substantial money.

There are no strict size requirements, but units larger than 30 square meters are preferred by lenders, as smaller units may limit options to cash buyers. If refinancing the whole building, different considerations apply. Prior approval applications cost £80, and for AFL members, we offer discounted rates through experienced planning consultants. Traditional planning applications can cost £350–£1,000 per unit and take up to two years, while prior approval takes just 56 days, offering a faster, more cost-effective alternative.

Once you have the planning consultant's view and have pre-mapped everything, you can have peace of mind and certainty that you are in safe territory. However, it is strongly advised to only exchange or complete a building with the planning application or permitted development rights from the council. Moreover, it is crucial to be aware of any covenants or specific regulations that may negatively impact the property, such as limitations on building in particular areas like mines or even restrictions on use.

There are no strict size requirements, but units larger than 30 square meters are preferred by lenders, as smaller units may limit options to cash buyers. If refinancing the whole building, different considerations apply. Prior approval applications cost £80, and for AFL members, we offer discounted rates through experienced planning consultants. Traditional planning applications can cost £350–£1,000 per unit and take up to two years, while prior approval takes just 56 days, offering a faster, more cost-effective alternative.

The Offer

Now, let's discuss the process of making an offer. It's essential to follow these guidelines without deviating. First and foremost, start by offering a lower amount if necessary, but be cautious to stay high as it may give the impression that you're not serious. Begin with a verbal offer to test the waters and gather information on how other parties respond. It's crucial to keep your emotions detached from the deal. The longer you invest in a project, the more attached you become. Therefore, it's best to set clear boundaries, and if an offer deviates from what you want, let it go. Avoid procuring a property that will not yield satisfactory returns, as your reputation in the industry depends on your success.

Maintain a profit margin of at least 25%, and staying within this percentage is advisable. Also, when evaluating the Gross Development Value (GDV), deduct a range of 5% to 10% to account for sensitivity analysis and worst-case scenarios such as declining market values and increased construction costs.

Always be prepared to back up your offer with proof of funding. This includes having a proven in-principle agreement for your financing. Building trust with commercial agents is essential to displaying professionalism and not divulging too much information. Be cautious when asked for floor plans or details about your plans for the building. Commercial agents may work with your competitors, and sharing all your ideas could jeopardise your deal. Politely decline to disclose sensitive information and hold your ground.

Instead of going back and forth via email, making the initial offer verbally is more effective. Request feedback on the vendor's expectations and if any other offers have been made for the project. This will help you better understand the seller's requirements and help you structure a competitive offer. Moving forward, there are a few more essential points to consider. Testing the waters can sometimes be tricky, as people may need to give you a direct answer. However, asking for a percentage range, such as 5% up or 5% down, can be helpful. This can give you a better understanding of their expectations.

Here's an important tip: it's best to send an offer via email and in writing. If you don't know the agent well, you should contact the vendor directly and address the offer to them, copying the agent. This ensures the vendor receives the offer and avoids misunderstandings or concerns about the agent's involvement. Conducting all necessary legal searches is essential between the offer exchange and completion.

Visit the site and familiarise yourself with the surroundings, ensuring that utilities and services are correct. You want to avoid buying a property that requires extensive studies or permissions to develop due to unforeseen issues like underground assets.

Secure funding and mortgages before starting your development. Obtain final construction drawings for accurate contractor pricing, and get budget estimates from multiple contractors to manage construction cost risks. Include a contingency in your budget and create a project risk register, covering surveys for rain, subsidence, asbestos, structural integrity, drainage, and soil viability. Ensure everything aligns before proceeding to avoid future issues, saving time, money, and frustration.

for a quick recap, remember planning is crucial when investing in property. It involves considering various aspects such as time, energy, and resources. Proper planning helps set realistic timelines for completing tasks, optimise energy usage, and allocate resources effectively. This ensures efficient project management and maximises productivity. In terms of property, planning plays a vital role in several areas. It involves selecting the right location based on market demand, proximity to amenities, and growth potential. Planning also includes conducting legal research and surveys to identify potential issues or restrictions affecting the property's development or use.

Furthermore, planning in property development involves securing funding and creating a financial plan to ensure adequate resources are available throughout the project. It also includes designing and producing architectural plans to meet functional and aesthetic requirements. Additionally, planning encompasses obtaining necessary permits and approvals from relevant authorities and ensuring compliance with building codes and regulations.

The power team, consisting of experts in various fields related to property development, is of utmost importance. These experts include architects, engineers, contractors, lawyers, and financial advisors who provide expertise and guidance throughout the planning and development process. The power team ensures that all aspects of the project are well-coordinated, risks are minimised, and the project progresses smoothly.

In summary, effective planning in property development involves considering time, energy, and resource management. It encompasses various aspects such as location selection, legal research, funding, architectural design, and compliance with regulations. Collaborating with a knowledgeable power team ensures a successful and well-executed property development project.

In Chapter 5, we cover key elements of a successful property development strategy, from building a power team to understanding planning permissions. Michele and Elisa's journey, from full-time employees to successful property entrepreneurs, showcases the importance of meticulous planning and strategic execution. Their HMO development success highlights the value of a clear vision, strong planning, and the right support. For more on their approach, check out the final chapter.

As we conclude this chapter, remember that planning is the cornerstone of successful property development. It's not just about securing planning permissions or constructing buildings; it's about envisioning your future, setting clear goals, and meticulously planning every step to achieve them. The importance of planning extends to building a power team, understanding regulations, managing your time effectively, and making informed financial decisions. Each component plays a vital role in shaping your property investment journey.

A well-structured plan guides you through the property market, ensuring legal compliance, resource optimization, and profitability. Focus on high-income tasks, delegate effectively, and stay organized to boost efficiency. Building a reliable power team of experts will streamline processes and amplify your success.

Embrace the planning phase with diligence and foresight. Let your vision drive your actions and maintain the discipline to follow through with your plans. With a solid plan and the right team, you can navigate the property market confidently, turning opportunities into profitable ventures and paving the way for long-term success.

Assignment

1. **Develop Your Vision:**
Write a clear three-year vision for your property business, including goals for the number of properties to manage, build, or sell, and your financial strategy.

2. **Assemble Your Power Team:**
Identify key members for your power team, such as planners, brokers, architects, builders, and solicitors. Research and list potential candidates or firms to approach.

3. **Create a Time Management Plan:**
Create a weekly schedule prioritizing high-income tasks like finding deals, networking, sales, and fundraising, while also allowing time for personal rest and balance.

4. **Understand Planning Permissions:**
Research local planning permission requirements, including the steps, timeframes, and costs for various developments.

5. **Evaluate Potential Development Sites:**
Evaluate a potential development site, considering location, market demand, regulations, and planning permissions. Summarize your findings and plan in a report.

6. **Engage with Experts:**
Meet with at least two professionals, like a planning consultant and architect, to discuss your vision and gather their feedback. Document their suggestions.

This assignment will strengthen your understanding of the planning process and the value of a strong power team, preparing you to take decisive, strategic actions for success in property development.

CHAPTER SIX

CONSTRUCTION

This chapter is significant, as it involves the highest level of risk in any development project, regardless of its size. Having a reliable and capable main contractor is crucial to the success of your development. Without a skilled contractor, the risk of project failure and potential disappointment is significantly higher. So, paying close attention to this chapter is vital to success.

Let me give you an overview of what we'll cover in this chapter. We'll start by discussing how to manage and oversee builders effectively, ensuring smooth communication and successful project execution. Then, we'll delve into different contracts and procurement strategies, enabling you to make informed decisions regarding your project. Lastly, we'll explore how the end product should be presented to make it attractive for selling or renting purposes.

Throughout this module, we'll provide detailed guidance and information to equip you with the knowledge and skills to navigate construction within property development successfully. So, let's dive in and ensure you're well-prepared to handle this critical aspect of your projects.

Procurement Strategy

Let's discuss the importance of constructing a procurement strategy for your construction activities within the property development process. This step is crucial in assembling an effective power team dedicated explicitly to construction-related tasks. By now, you should have acquired the site and engaged professionals like solicitors and accountants.

Developing an effective procurement strategy is vital for the success of your construction activities in the property development process. However, for the construction aspect, it is crucial to focus on the following key individuals:

1. **Chartered Architect and Planning Consultant:** While architects provide sketches and construction drawings, they may not specialise in obtaining planning permissions. Hiring a planning consultant with a track record of securing planning permissions is advisable. This investment can save you time and money in the long run.

2. **Chartered Structural/Civil Engineer:** These professionals are responsible for designing foundations, substructures, superstructures, and drainage systems. It is essential to engage a firm with in-house expertise in these areas. Opting for chartered engineers ensures a certain level of competence and adherence to professional standards. Additionally, ensure they have professional indemnity insurance to cover potential errors.

3. **Mechanical and Electrical Engineers:** Depending on the complexity of your project, you may need to involve these experts for services such as boilers, lifts, and electrical power systems. Their involvement is crucial for more intricate projects. Remember that their fees can vary based on the scope of work required.

4. **Quantity Surveyor:** This professional oversees cost management and takes responsibility for monitoring project expenses. Their expertise ensures effective budget control throughout the construction phase.

By carefully selecting and coordinating these power team members, you can ensure a smooth and successful construction phase in your property development project.

It is crucial to have a written agreement signed by the quantity surveyor to ensure a smooth process. However, one critical aspect developers often overlook is the role of subcontractors. As leading contractors with years of experience, we want to emphasise that subcontractors' performance significantly impacts a project's success. Delays mainly occur due to poor performance by subcontractors. As the main contractor, you bear the responsibility when delays happen. To mitigate this risk, it is essential to carefully scrutinise the subcontractor list and provide it to the main contractor. We usually have a separate agreement with the subcontractors, allowing me to step in and take over their work if necessary. This approach has saved us a lot of time and money.

While some main contractors may not prefer this arrangement, we make it compulsory. Remember, as the developer, you hold the power and financial resources.

Before Appointment

Before your appointment with any main contractors, there are some crucial steps you should take. Firstly, it is recommended that you prepare a comprehensive work schedule with quantities and as much detail as possible, down to the millimetre. This ensures that you can accurately compare quotes from different contractors and avoid costly pricing mistakes. You should also prepare a set of construction drawings with your architect, interior designer, and contractor, covering everything from demolition to finishes. This will help you delegate tasks to builders and subcontractors and maintain a clear timeline for the project.

Next, you must choose a standard form of contract such as JCT or NEC, opting for a lump-sum contract wherever possible to pass risk to the main contractor. You should also decide between a traditional or design-and-build approach. The former involves hiring separate contractors for each project stage, while the latter involves a single contractor handling the entire process from design to construction. Taking these steps before your appointment will put you in a solid position to negotiate with the main contractors and ensure a successful, cost-effective project.

A managing contract option is appointing a project manager who packages the project into sections and procures packages individually. While this approach is sometimes risky, it is commonly used for larger projects. However, choosing either a design and build or a traditional approach is generally recommended.

To ensure you fulfil your responsibilities as a client, it is essential to familiarise yourself with the Construction Design and Management Regulations 2015 (CDM regulations). These regulations outline your responsibilities and ensure the safety and health of all project stakeholders. Therefore, it is essential to understand and comply with these regulations.

Program of Works

Having a program of work is an essential component of any project. It helps monitor the efficiency of the main contractor and ensures that the project is completed on schedule. It is advisable to speak to someone who works with programs of works daily to understand their significance fully.

Programs of work are essential for medium to larger projects and should not be overlooked. While it's possible to create a program that works in Excel, using specialized software like Primavera is recommended. The program comprises a summary of all the activities required for the project, with a duration and finish date specified for each. The horizontal bars represent a specific period needed to complete that activity for the project.

When monitoring progress while on-site, every given point should have a line drawn through it. This ensures that the site is on schedule with the program of work. If not, you need to ask the contractor what is causing the delay and take corrective action. Additionally, get your contractor to give you a program of work for the next two weeks and what materials and resources will be required to complete them. These measures will put you in a better position to manage your project effectively and ensure it is delivered on time.

Ensuring you have all the necessary documents and materials organised adequately for your project is essential. This includes considering the critical path, which consists of the vital activities that must be carried out to keep the project moving forward. Some examples of essential activities include planning and laying foundations, without which the project cannot progress.

It is also crucial to set a target project completion date. In the scenario presented, the completion date is set for December 6th. It is advisable to seek professional help for medium-sized projects to ensure the work program is developed correctly. In some cases, the main contractor for a design-build contract may be able to assist with this. It is worth noting that other programs, such as Microsoft Project and others, are available in addition to Primavera.

Where To Find Builders for Small/Medium Projects

This section will discuss how to find builders for small and medium-sized projects as SME developers. We often undertake small refurbishments and medium-sized projects, typically 16-25 units. We have often been asked where to find reliable and trustworthy builders with whom to build a good rapport. We have compiled a list of options for you.

A highly recommended resource for small projects is the "Rated People" app, where you can find builders with good ratings. I found my first builder using this app, but remember to meticulously scrutinise their reviews to ensure authenticity. Additionally, local newspapers often feature advertisements for builders.

Contacting building control companies is another excellent option. These companies constantly monitor the quality of leading contractors and builders, making them a reliable source for finding reputable builders. Simply explain your requirement for a reputable builder, emphasising your preference for professionals over amateurs or subpar contractors.

Architects and planning consultants can also be a valuable resource. However, ensure that these professionals are familiar with the specific requirements of your project. for instance, if you plan a residential, commercial storage, or conversion project, ensure that your architect or planning consultant specializes in these areas. Their expertise may not be suitable for new builds.

Participating in Facebook groups and other social media platforms dedicated to property development can provide valuable insights and feedback from fellow developers. Additionally, consider utilising LinkedIn to connect with local builders and explore potential collaborations.

Attending networking events tailored explicitly to property development is another effective strategy. We often attend the London Developers Club, a monthly gathering where like-minded developers meet and mingle. These events create opportunities to connect with other developers and contractors, facilitating potential partnerships.

Working With Builders

To ensure you appoint a good contractor, follow these steps and strategies. Many people ask me how to choose a reliable contractor, so here are my recommended steps:

Step 1: Shortlist Contractors

For larger projects, prepare a pre-tender document. Send this document to potential contractors and request information about their recent projects, current clients, on-site projects, and insurance coverage details. Once you receive their responses, create a pre-qualification list and select five or seven contractors for further evaluation.

Step 2: Phone Interviews

Arrange phone calls with the selected contractors to scrutinize their experience and determine if you are satisfied with them as the main contractor. Inform them you are securing funding for the project, even if it has not been finalised yet. This helps gauge their level of interest and commitment.

Step 3: Request References

Ask the main contractors for at least five referees who can speak to their previous work. It is crucial to visit these projects to confirm that the contractors provide genuine references and evaluate their workmanship. Additionally, contact a structural engineer, a building control company, and an architect who has worked with the contractor to verify their credibility.

Step 4: Check Background

Review the contractor's track record on Companies House, ensuring they have been in operation for a considerable duration. Look for contractors with several years of experience, which indicates they have acquired knowledge and skills over time. Remember to assess their specific expertise related to your project.

Step 5: On-Site Management

Inquire if the main contractor will personally be working on-site. Small companies often have their managing director involved in the project, which can result in faster and smoother progress. Having the managing director work directly on-site is advantageous.

Remember to adapt these steps to your project's requirements and ensure that the contractor possesses relevant experience in the specific construction aspect you are targeting.

Following these steps can increase the likelihood of appointing a reputable and capable contractor for your project.

When selecting a contractor, it's essential to have clear communication with them. Email them all the necessary drawings, quantities, specifications, and other project details. Give them a deadline to respond and invite them to visit the site. A site visit is crucial because it allows the contractor to assess its accessibility and consider any logistical challenges.

During the site visit, ask the contractor detailed questions about how they plan to complete the project. Discuss the project schedule and confirm if they have the necessary resources to meet your timeline. Additionally, ask about their current workload to ensure they can dedicate sufficient attention to your project.

Requesting permission to visit one of their current projects can also be beneficial. This visit will allow you to see how the contractor operates, assess their organization and cleanliness on-site, and gain insights into the company's culture.

Furthermore, the location of the contractor and their staff should be considered. If they are located far away from the project site, it may result in delays and potential fatigue during daily travel. Considering all these factors will help you make an informed decision when selecting a contractor.

To ensure the smooth execution of the project, it is essential to consider the contractor's proximity to the site and their accommodation arrangements if they are not local. Train or transportation options to the site should also be discussed, especially if parking space or public transport is limited.

Meet the project manager face-to-face during the selection process and evaluate their qualifications and suitability. Knowing if the contractor has experience working with local subcontractors is also beneficial as this indicates good communication and established relationships. Inquire about the largest subcontractors, their relationship with the main contractor, and their contact details for reference.

Moving on to step three, it is recommended to shortlist and evaluate a minimum of three main contractors. When faced with multiple contractors of similar expertise, experience, and pricing, the key deciding factor should be the project manager. Interview the project manager to assess their competency and fit for the project.

In the construction industry, success often relies on personal relationships and effective communication. Therefore, the project manager's qualities and alignment with your objectives should be considered when making a final decision.

There are different types of project managers in construction, just like there are various types of light bulbs. Some project managers are passionate, energetic, and highly involved, while others may be less engaged. When selecting a main contractor, meeting the project manager face-to-face and gauging their enthusiasm and commitment to your project is crucial. In such cases, it is recommended to prioritise choosing a company based on the quality of their project manager rather than solely focusing on cost and capacity. This ensures that your project will be delivered on budget and, ideally, on target.

Once you have selected the main contractor, it is essential to have a written contract in place. The contract should be clear and straightforward, minimising any potential misinterpretations. Various contract types are available, such as JCT conditional contracts and NAC conditional contracts. It is essential to have a specialist, such as a lawyer or a Quantity Surveyor, to help you navigate the complexities of these contracts. Additionally, the contract should include agreements regarding the project timeline and any penalties for delays, such as liquidated damages.

Moving on to step four, setting up regular site meetings, preferably every week is advisable. These meetings are crucial for monitoring the project's progress and ensuring the main contractor does not cut corners or compromise quality. Site meetings also allow for early detection and resolution of any issues. Just as children require constant attention, your project needs consistent oversight. If you don't have the resources to attend the meetings yourself, delegating this responsibility to a project manager or someone you trust is essential.

Furthermore, it is essential to establish a schedule of payments for the project. However, it is important to exercise caution and not make a payment of more than 2% of the total project value at the start. This ensures that you maintain control and protect your financial interests.

We hope these points clarify the importance of project managers, contracts, site meetings, and payment schedules.

It is expected to encounter untrustworthy contractors who demand upfront payment, even half the total cost. In such situations, rejecting their offer and seeking other reliable contractors is advisable. It is important to question why they require such a significant upfront payment.

We had a similar experience with a main contractor handling a demolition project. They also wanted a large upfront payment for a relatively small project costing 55,000 pounds. We questioned their need for such an amount, pointing out that expenses like renting a scrap yard, which we estimated to cost around 350-400 pounds, including VAT, should not require such a substantial payment. We clarified that we would only provide 100 pounds initially, with the rest to be paid based on progress. It is crucial to stand your ground and not be swayed by their demands.

When invoicing for refurbishment projects, ensuring that the main contractor invoices you for "replacement, repair, or renew" work is crucial. This wording allows you to offset the refurbishment costs as expenses when paying taxes. This can result in paying little to no taxes on the project, which is advantageous. for instance, if a refurbishment project costs 55,000 pounds, you would only be liable to pay taxes after you have recouped all your expenses.

Photographing the progress of your project is vital for building control purposes and for your records. We can illustrate this with another example. We completed a site at the end of 2017, and the 10-year insurance provider asked for evidence of the movement joints installed during the superstructure construction. Initially, we thought it was a joke since we had lost our records. fortunately, we had instructed our main contractor to document the project with videos and photographs regularly. We provided this evidence to the insurance company, assuring them that the correct joints were installed. As a result, we were granted a 10-year warranty. Having a record of such projects is crucial, as they serve as valuable references for your CV and promotional materials.

So, remember to document your projects through photos and videos, both for adherence to building control regulations and for building your record. Maintaining accurate records for your showcasing purposes, such as brochures and portfolios, is also essential.

Maintaining accurate records of your property units is essential, especially if you plan to keep them. These records will help you in cases of leaks or pipe damage, as they will provide information on the layout and location of pipes. This documentation can prove to be invaluable when addressing these types of issues.

Additionally, requesting As-built drawings from contractors if they deviate from the original construction drawings is advisable. In many cases, the architect will provide comprehensive construction drawings to the main contractor, but it is common for the contractor to identify the need for changes. To ensure you have the accurate information, ask the main contractor to provide As-built drawings that accurately reflect the modified plans. With these drawings, you can clearly understand the project's finished state, which will be helpful if any problems arise in the future.

Before proceeding to the next step, we encourage you to take a break, drink, or enjoy a cup of coffee. It's essential to stay refreshed. We will be here when you are ready to continue.

Now, let's move on to step number five. One crucial aspect is to consult with your accountant to ensure you have the best possible exit strategy and minimise your tax liabilities. It is advisable to have this discussion early on to determine the most effective structure for your investment.

Don't forget all that we have previously advised you to keep in mind, from asking your main contractor to invoice you for "replacement, repair, or renew" work, documenting your projects through photos and videos and requesting As-built drawings from contractors.

Lastly, it is vital to start looking for your next deal while still working on your current project. Securing the next opportunity can take time, so it's wise to keep your focus on analysing potential deals and planning for growth.

Interior Finishes

Alright, let's dive into interior finishes. We want to share some valuable tips with you. When it comes to interior design, remember that you are selling a lifestyle. The more boxes you can check for your customers, the more likely they are to choose you. So, it's important to answer these three important questions.

First, what do your customers want and need? Understanding their desires and requirements is key. Secondly, why should they choose you over others? What sets you apart? Lastly, how can you transform their space or provide something unique that they can't resist?

By answering these questions, you can create a powerful product that customers won't be able to resist. We have some valuable insights to share with you based on the types of products we produce for our rental units, new builds, and commercial conversions.

One strategy we use is feature walls. We know that painting walls nicely is not a priority for every developer, but we take the time to create attractive feature walls with neutral colors that give our properties a modern look. Additionally, we strategically use mirrors to create the illusion of larger rooms by reflecting light.

To enhance the visual appeal further, we incorporate photographs, cushions, lamps, and stylish furniture. Empty rooms can be difficult for potential tenants to envision, but with well-furnished spaces, they can truly see the potential. for our HMO properties, fusion furniture has been a reliable choice. They offer quality furniture options at reasonable prices and even provide on-site cutouts, making the process hassle-free.

To give you an idea, we would like to show you some pictures of our previous projects. These photos are from our first-ever HMO that we built a few years ago at the beginning of our journey. Since then, we have raised the standard and achieved even better results. The bright and fresh ambiance you see in the pictures is what we strive to create with our interior finishes.

We hope these ideas and insights will inspire you as you navigate through interior finishes. Now, let's move on to the next section.

Here, you can get a glimpse of the furniture we carefully choose for these sites. We believe in creating spaces that resonate with our target audience.

Now, let me present you with a prime example of our latest project. This is one of our HMOs in Ipswich 5 bed all ensuites. I must admit, it's a place that we would gladly call home. From the elegant mirrors to the charming lamps and unique features, we want every tenant to feel proud and excited to live there.

We’re confident that these examples have provided you with a clear understanding of our approach. Now, it's your turn to take all the knowledge we've shared and apply it to your own projects. Good luck, and may your endeavors be successful!

This chapter underscores the importance of managing the most critical and risk-laden aspect of property development: construction. From selecting a reliable main contractor to executing a comprehensive procurement strategy, every detail matters. The success of your development project hinges on your ability to oversee builders effectively, make informed contractual decisions, and present a high-quality end product.

Navigating the construction phase requires a well-coordinated power team. By engaging chartered professionals such as architects, engineers, and quantity surveyors, you ensure that your project adheres to the highest standards and mitigates potential risks. The strategic selection and management of subcontractors further bolster the project's success, preventing costly delays and ensuring smooth operations.

Effective project management requires planning, clear communication, and regular site visits to ensure progress and quality. Adhering to regulations and maintaining accurate documentation are crucial. Focus on detailed planning, managing contractors, and delivering quality finishes to stand out. Stay diligent, focused, and leverage your team's expertise to turn challenges into opportunities.

ASSIGNMENT

Create a list of 10 local builders and contractors through site visits, online research, or other methods. Focus on finding local quantity surveyors (QSS) who understand costs and work closely with builders. Speak with at least three QSS to gather information on the cost per square meter for timber frame, traditional block work, and alternative methods like steel.

Another task is to compile a list of local building control companies. Network and ask for recommendations in Facebook groups, local communities, or networking events. Specifically, look into LMPG (Local Authority Building Control) membership and the benefits it offers. LMPG provides amazing discounts, which can lead to substantial savings. for example, we saved approximately £500 on a boiler by leveraging the discounts available through our LMPG membership.

To deepen your understanding of project management, we recommend shadowing a project manager or your mentor during a progress meeting on a construction site. Ask as many questions as possible and actively participate in the meeting. This experience will provide insights into the day-to-day tasks and responsibilities of project managers.

We are confident that you now have a clear understanding of your assignment. Apply all the knowledge you've gained and good luck!

CHAPTER SEVEN

EXIT STRATEGY

We have reached the final step, which focuses on the exit strategy. We will cover various aspects of refinancing your property, strategies to achieve the bestselling and rental prices, tax implications, and we will share some valuable top tips with you.

Requirements for success:

Let's begin with the first lesson of this chapter, where we discuss the requirements for achieving a successful exit. It is crucial to follow the correct process to ensure the asset, whether it's a property or any other project, is a success. One key aspect is ensuring that what you have produced is in demand and meets the needs of the market. Without fulfilling these requirements, your exit may not yield favourable results.

Furthermore, always strive to work to a high standard. Remember, cheaper is not always better. While it is important to cut costs and streamline your projects, it is equally important to deliver a product or service of exceptional quality. Going above and beyond for your investors, tenants, and local communities is something we strongly believe in. To be recognised as the best landlords in your area, you need to invest in the best and set yourself apart from the competition. Taking great photos is essential, as visuals play a significant role in attracting potential investors and tenants. While smartphones can produce excellent photos, consider hiring a professional photographer. You can contact local universities or colleges to find photography students who may be interested in using your property for their portfolio. Alternatively, you can enlist the services of a reasonably priced professional photographer.

Additionally, we encourage you to document your projects through videos. Record the before, during, and after stages of each project. These videos serve multiple purposes: they provide a valuable reference for future projects, allow you to showcase your work to investors, and inspire others. By documenting your projects, you create social proof and establish your brand and reputation. Utilise these videos on your website and social media channels to enhance your credibility and become the go-to person in your field.

Remember, maintaining records of your projects' progress is crucial. Leverage these videos and information to attract investors, build your brand, and motivate others. By demonstrating your success and expertise, you will become a credible figure in your industry. These are key points to consider when it comes to planning your exit strategy.

Tax (We are NOT Tax Advisers)

While we cannot avoid taxes entirely, we can strive to earn more while paying less in the most efficient tax structure possible. To achieve this, it is crucial to consult a property tax accountant.

Ensure that the person you work with specialises in property taxation. If you are purchasing property through a limited company, it is important to be aware of corporation tax, which is levied on your profits. However, one advantage of having a limited company is the ability to write off legitimate business expenses such as fuel, mobile phone expenses, business-related purchases, travel expenses, and business lunches against your corporation tax. Additionally, training and mentoring costs can be paid by the company. Thus, establishing a limited company can be highly beneficial.

Capital gains tax is another important tax to consider. It is essential to have the correct tax structure in place from the beginning. for every new deal, joint venture partnership, or new strategy we undertake, we always consult our tax advisors first. We provide them with details about our plans, the parties involved (investors, shareholders, directors), the flow of money, and how profits will be shared. It is crucial to always seek advice from your tax advisor, as everyone's situation is different.

As we are not tax advisors, it would be inappropriate for us to provide detailed advice. However, my recommendation is to utilise the services of a property tax accountant to set up your businesses and ensure they are structured in the most tax-efficient way. There are legal channels and various methods available to help you earn more and pay less in taxes, ultimately providing the cash flow you desire for reinvestment in your business.

Remember, taxes are an integral part of business ownership, and seeking professional guidance is essential to navigate the complexities of the tax system.

Selling units

Let's discuss the steps you can take as a professional property investor to ensure a successful sale of your units. A key tip is to engage selling agents who can provide an estimate of the selling price and identify potential buyers for your units. They can also evaluate your floor plans. Typically, agent fees range from one to one and a half percent. To sell your units effectively, consider obtaining an Energy Performance Certificate (EPC), hosting open days and weekends, and showcasing well-dressed units. Creating a sales brochure and exploring options like Help to Buy can also enhance your selling prospects.

It is important to stay informed about the current qualification criteria and price limits for Help to Buy, as these may vary based on location. Additionally, you will need to budget for solicitor fees, which typically amount to around £750 per property sale.

As a property investor, it is crucial to not only focus on building, converting, and purchasing properties, but also consider the exit strategy. By employing these top tips, such as dressing the units and understanding customer preferences, working with reputable agents, and ensuring contractual flexibility, you can achieve a quick and profitable sale.

Remember, it is worth investing in the best services when you aim for the best results.

Re-financing

Here we are, moving on to the next section where we will discuss refinancing. It is essential to ensure that you obtain the best possible mortgage and valuation. To achieve this, working with a competent mortgage advisor is crucial. David Tonks, one of our trusted mortgage advisors, has been assisting many of our Academy graduates and building strong relationships with them. If feasible, consider refinancing with a commercial mortgage. A commercial mortgage values the asset based on its rental income rather than its physical structure. for instance, a well-converted and properly equipped HMO (House in Multiple Occupation) can be assessed commercially. Commercial valuations are advantageous because a higher valuation offers a greater chance of retrieving the original investment, including the deposit and refurbishment costs. This strategy may not be applicable to single-let properties but works well for aspiring HMO investors.

Some recommended lenders for commercial valuations include Shawbrook, Lloyds Commercial, Cambridge & Counties Bank, and Metro Bank. It is highly recommended to work with a broker throughout this process. Here is a rough formula we use to estimate commercial valuations: start by deducting 20% from the gross yearly rental income to account for voids and bad debt. Next, multiply the adjusted figure by 10 (or another appropriate valuation multiple). This will give you the potential commercial value of the property. However, bear in mind that they will not lend you 100% of the commercial value. Previous lessons emphasised that you may typically receive a 75% loan-to-value mortgage. So, multiply the new value by 75% to determine the potential mortgage amount the bank will lend you.

Keep in mind that this formula is simply a guide and actual valuations may differ. Prepare all the necessary documentation and collate relevant information for the valuer. When you are ready to refinance, contact your mortgage broker, like David Tonks, and inform them about your intention to seek refinancing. They will then find the best lender that suits your requirements. The lender will then appoint a surveyor to inspect the property. It is highly recommended that you be present during the survey as it allows you to showcase your professionalism, discuss the quality of work, and highlight any improvements made. Provide the surveyor with a schedule or program of works, explaining in detail the investments you have made in the property for its conversion.

Remember, manipulating surveys is not possible, and surveyors can be challenging to work with at times. A helpful tip is to maintain a professional demeanor and engage with the surveyor during the property inspection to ensure transparency. Aim to portray your property investment as a legitimate business rather than a hobby.

When undertaking a high HMO conversion to achieve commercial value, there are a few important factors to consider. First, ensure that the property cannot be easily converted back into a single dwelling and aim for as many en-suite rooms as possible.

There are two refinancing options. Option one involves getting an uplift with the same lender. After adding value to the property, the lender conducts a new valuation. If the value has increased, you can obtain a second mortgage. Benefits include familiarity with the lender, reduced due diligence, and potentially better rates. However, a six-month ownership rule may apply, and the value uplift might be lower than with a different lender or surveyor.

Option two is commercial refinancing, which bypasses the six-month rule and allows immediate refinancing if property value has increased. It offers the potential to pull out all invested capital and scale investments with lenders like Shawbrook. However, commercial survey fees are higher (£1,000–£1,500), and interest rates tend to be higher. To achieve a free development, you need an increase of 125–143% of total costs, depending on the loan-to-value ratio. While higher LTV ratios require a lower value increase, they come with higher leverage.

In conclusion, when exploring refinancing options, it is advisable to consult one or two brokers who can understand your goals and search the market for suitable options. A knowledgeable and experienced mortgage broker, like David Tonks, can be an essential part of your power team for success in property investment.

Land deal

This case study examines a land development project in Colchester Town Centre. The land, purchased for £310,750, had planning approval for nine dwellings. Total development costs, including professional fees and interest, amounted to £1.5 million. The Gross Development Value (GDV) was £2 million, resulting in a profit of £492,000, or 25% of GDP.

The initial plan was to refinance the property, which would have left £7,901 in the deal. However, due to investor preferences and site complications, the decision was made to sell the units. While the profit was lower than projected, the project was still successful as all units were sold. This case emphasizes the importance of having multiple exit strategies, being flexible, and preparing for unexpected challenges and market fluctuations.

HMO- Re-Finance

For this section we will examine one of our highly successful HMO (House in Multiple Occupation) projects and discuss the refinancing process. The property in focus is located at 42 Old Heath Road, and it has met all the criteria and principles we have taught you throughout the modules.

The initial purchase of the property was £160,000, with an additional £50,000 invested in refurbishments. A joint venture partner contributed £210,000 to the project. We rented out the five rooms at a rate of £500 each, resulting in a monthly income of £2,500 and an annual income of £30,000. Now, the next decision was whether to refinance commercially or pursue an uplift in the bricks and mortar value with the same lender.

Considering the property's commercial value , we anticipated it to be approximately £240,000, similar to what we could achieve through a commercial equation. Therefore, opting to stay with the same lender seemed favorable, as it saved us costs, facilitated a faster process, and allowed for an 85% loan-to-value mortgage, compared to a 75% loan-to-value mortgage for a commercial appraisal. Although the commercial value might have been slightly lower, the ability to borrow at a higher percentage resulted in us pulling out a similar amount of money while securing a better mortgage deal. Overall, we only left £6,000 in the deal, which is a significant achievement.

Despite not retrieving all the invested funds, the project generates a profit split of approximately £11,125. With five rooms rented at £500 each and a mortgage interest rate of 5%, after deducting bills and maintenance expenses, we are left with a profit of £562 per month. This showcases the ability to generate a fantastic deal and highlights various considerations for the exit strategy. In this particular case, returning to the same lender and successfully refinancing allowed us to potentially include this property in our portfolio indefinitely. It has been a part of our portfolio for around four and a half years (at the time of writing this book), and it continues to provide high cash flow with excellent tenants. Although we have not fully withdrawn all the initial investment, the rental income allows us to recoup our funds and build equity over time. This example demonstrates the potential to add similar deals in your own portfolio.

Repaying Investors

Repaying investors promptly and transparently is key to maintaining trust and building long-term partnerships. Here's how to manage the repayment process effectively:

Plan for Repayment

1. **Clear Agreements:** From the outset, have clear, written agreements detailing how and when investors will be repaid. This includes the terms of investment, the expected return, and the timeline for repayment.
2. **Regular Updates:** Keep your investors informed about the progress of the project. Regular updates help maintain transparency and trust. This can be done through monthly reports, emails, or meetings.
3. **Structured Payments:** Structure the repayment process according to the project's cash flow. This might include periodic interest payments during the project and the return of the principal upon completion or sale.
4. **Contingency Planning:** Have a contingency plan in place. Sometimes, projects can face delays or unforeseen costs. Having a buffer or alternative repayment plan ensures that you can still meet your obligations to investors.

Process of Repayment

1. **Completion and Valuation:** Upon completing the project, conduct a thorough valuation to determine its current market value. This step is crucial whether you're refinancing or selling the property.
2. **Refinancing:** If you opt to refinance, ensure you have the best possible mortgage terms. The proceeds from the refinancing can be used to repay the investors. Ensure the new mortgage aligns with your long-term investment strategy.
3. **Sale of Units:** If selling the units, work with experienced Estate Agents to achieve the best possible price. The proceeds from the sales should first cover any outstanding debts, including payments to investors.

4. **Final Settlement:** Once the proceeds are in, distribute the returns to investors according to the agreed terms. Ensure all financial transactions are documented and communicated clearly to the investors.

By adhering to these guidelines, you not only fulfill your financial obligations but also strengthen your reputation as a reliable and trustworthy developer. This paves the way for future collaborations and investments.

Shaun Bartle, a qualified accountant and tax firm owner, was trading time for money without equity in his business. Realising his corporate success didn't fulfill his aspirations, he joined Assets for Life (AFL). Through mentorship, Shaun discovered joint venture finance and raised over £320k, completing seven property deals. One key achievement was a no-money-down flip deal, which kickstarted his ongoing success.

Shaun's journey highlights the importance of a clear exit strategy and mentorship in achieving financial freedom. His transition from a corporate accountant to a successful property investor shows the power of a well-planned exit and the right guidance. Learn more about his story in the final chapter of this book.

Congratulations on reaching the final step in your property development journey! Your exit strategy is a vital component of your project's success. By focusing on high standards, understanding market demands, and leveraging professional advice, you can maximize your returns and solidify your reputation in the industry.

A successful exit strategy involves meeting market demands, maintaining strong investor relationships, and establishing credibility as a developer. By delivering quality projects, documenting success, and managing taxes, you ensure long-term growth and profitability.

Remember, the journey doesn't end here. Continue to refine your strategies, build robust networks, and stay informed about market trends. Your commitment to excellence will drive your success in the competitive world of property development.

Assignment

1. **Evaluate Market Demand:**
Research and document the current market demands for your property type. What are potential buyers or tenants looking for? How does your property meet these needs?

2. **Professional Photography and Videography:**
Hire a professional photographer or collaborate with local universities to document your project. Create a portfolio of high-quality photos and videos showcasing the before, during, and after stages of your development.

3. **Tax Consultation:**
Schedule a meeting with a property tax accountant. Discuss the best tax structures for your business and ensure you understand the implications of your exit strategy on your tax obligations.

4. **Selling Strategy:**
Engage with Estate Agents to get an estimate of the selling price and potential buyers for your units. Create a detailed plan for open days, marketing materials, and promotional strategies.

5. **Refinancing Plan:**
Consult with a mortgage broker to explore refinancing options. Prepare all necessary documentation and schedule a property valuation. Develop a plan for either a commercial mortgage or an uplift with the same lender.

6. **Repayment Strategy:**
Develop a detailed repayment plan for your investors. Outline the repayment timeline, structure, and contingency plans. Ensure that all agreements are documented and communicated clearly.

By completing this assignment, you will solidify your understanding of the exit strategy and be well-prepared to maximize your returns and achieve long-term success in property development.

BONUS CHAPTER

BUSINESS FUNDAMENTALS

Reading through this book, it is really important that you put into practice some of what you have learnt, as having the information and not taking the steps will not get you anywhere. The fact that you are even reading this book tells us that you are somewhat of an action taker, so don't hesitate or keep waiting for the perfect moment because that may never come.

So, in this chapter we are going to be looking at the business fundamentals, how to set up your business. The systems and processes that you can use in your property business to go and make lots of money and find quality deals. Because ultimately, if you treat it like a business, it will pay you like one, and if you set it up correctly from the beginning, then you can leverage people's time and knowledge. You can leverage systems and processes because you know the reason why you have chosen this business. We do not know about you but we got into property because we wanted more time and freedom. Yes, we want the financial freedom but we also need the time freedom to do what it is that we truly desire, which is to train thousands of people through our programs, enabling them to also experience success.

Setting up your business in the beginning is really going to help you grow and it will ultimately help you have more time to do the things that you love, so this is going to be a very powerful step that you are about to take.

VALUES

What we are going to share with you now is something very powerful, because you have to have the right mindset when it comes to making money. This was something that was shared with us years ago and we have spoken at length about this in chapter two. We are now going to share with you some information that we teach our clients in what we call the Wealth formula.

We are touching on value here in the business fundamentals because your inner worth as someone who is starting out in business is very important, this is the value you give to yourself, times the outer worth, which is the value to others and that will equal your net worth. Now most people, and maybe you can relate to this, don't value themselves enough. And if you don't value yourself enough, you're never going to go out there and do the things that you need to do and make the money that you want to make. You need to get in tune with yourself as a person. What do you stand for? What do you stand against? What do you bring to the table? What are all your assets? Then you've got to give value to other people, but here's the thing, if you've got net worth, what you really want is sustained wealth, and how you get sustained wealth is money focused .

So, you've got to learn how to manage your money, how to focus on making profits, not just turnover, and then you've got to learn how to invest that money correctly. Now, there are a lot of jobs out there, or businesses where you can make a lot of money fast, right? There are numerous business ideas that you can venture into but what is crucial is, what will be sustainable?

We believe it is then essential to get involved in something that has a positive impact, something that also has the ability to turn your focus on to other people. Now, in order to do that you have to be selfish to become selfless, it sounds harsh, but it is a solid fact. You are the number one priority right now, going through the property business accelerator is the most important thing in your life. Because once you've been through this training, once you go out there and implement the work, you will get the results. And then once you've got yourself set up, you can then go out there and help other people. The more people you serve, the more problems you solve and, the bigger your bank balance. Your bank balance is in direct relation to the number of people you serve, so start serving more people. When you build a property business, you are serving local communities, you are helping investors, you are putting good into the world, you are providing a great service and ultimately, that's how you start to make more money - very powerful. When we come into the practice of selfless service, we simultaneously feed our own self-worth and value. Giving to others is more than just volunteering; it's offering something of ourselves that is uniquely precious and our own.

If you are wondering what the difference between self-love and self-value are, well, self-value is more behavioural as opposed to self-love which is more emotional. This is where we take the foundation of how we feel about ourselves and put it to work. Self-value is the driving vehicle that allows us to walk the walk and act in ways that align with what we value and enables us to treat our team the same way. Our self-value shows up in the way we talk to people or in steps we take to speak our truth.

Valuing others within your business is also vital to the success of your organisation. It's very important to show that you value your team members; we believe we all like to be valued and our team members are no exception. You have to ensure you recognise that the people who make up your team are not just numbers but people that bring something unique to the table. Having the right people on board and treating them with respect goes a long way in your ability to make your business grow. However, the truth is that unless you value yourself and your business then you won't put value on your team.
One of our first values within our training module is QUALITY. We don't know about you, but we want an exceptional life, we want the finer things in life, everything we do, we want to do it to the best of our ability. Therefore, we want to provide exceptional quality and value to our investors, tenants, partners, clients that we are training and our people that work in the Assets for Life team. We want to be known as the best landlords, providing the best rooms in our local communities. If you are going to do something, do it properly, do not cut corners, go above and beyond and provide a quality five-star service.

TRUST is another strong value of ours, we are a bit old school so if we look into your eyes, put our hand out to shake your hand and we go into deals or we agree on negotiation, we stand by it. Integrity is key.

Now, PARTNERSHIP is another area that we value tremendously, it's really important that you have the right shareholder agreements in place of JV agreements, and you don't just do business on a handshake but you also want to be supportive of other people and it's very, very easy to let people down, so be integral. If you say you're going to be somewhere at nine o'clock, be there at the latest quarter to nine, if you say you're going to call someone at 10 o'clock, call them at 10 o'clock, if you say you're going to do something for someone, do it. We all fall short from time to time, right? If you ever fall short, hold your hands up, take responsibility, this is an essential value in your business.

You cannot do this all on your own, allow people to come into your business, we are always looking for new business partners, and hey, there's no reason why we can't become your next business partner too at some point in the future. We like to do collaborations, so for us, partnership is a real core value. We respect one doing what they say they are going to do. In business you need to have care and love for people, treat them how you want to be treated and respect them at all times.

Another area of value is DEDICATION, this is another essential value in our company Assets for Life, we have got this drive and enthusiasm to stay dedicated to the cause. We make a promise to people and we want to be dedicated to seeing those promises through. We will do anything that we need to do in order to help those who have trusted us to get the results they desire. The last value is INSPIRATION and you reading this book inspires us to go further. Sometimes it is the little steps that bring about the biggest change. Let us talk you through the values, the mission, the vision and the legacy as everything comes together. After reading this book, over the next few weeks or months, you are going to need to make some decisions and sometimes these decisions can be hard.

We had a situation a couple of years ago, where we were introduced to a high-net-worth investor in London. This guy was extremely wealthy, he was a multi-millionaire. We were looking for him to become one of our JV partners, so we spent some time with him going into London being driven around in a real fancy Rolls Royce and going to posh restaurants. After about three or four meetups with this guy, we were in a bit of a situation because he literally said to us, "I'm gonna start with 2 million pounds. If you get a good result on 2 million pounds, there's plenty more."

We really liked the sound of that and we were keen to make this guy some money, but the bottom line was, honestly, he was a bit of a dick. He was a bit more than a bit of a dick. He was a complete idiot. He was rude and controlling and we just thought to ourselves, you know what, if we take this guy's money, he's going to think he owns us and so we made a decision. We went back to our values and it didn't fit with the values of the company. It is extremely important to have strong values. You've got to understand what you stand for and what you stand against. Your vision is ultimately going to keep you on track. So, your mission will lead you to your vision and your vision or goal leads you to your legacy.

At all times you have got to start with the end in mind, you might not be a professional property investor for the rest of your life, but you've got to go into this with the mindset that this is going to become something very special, it's going to become something that you can be proud of, it's going to become something that you can really scale and grow. And perhaps leave a really strong legacy behind, for your children and loved ones. So, always start with the end in mind and think about being in for the long haul. This is why laying the correct foundation is vital. We are going to go through all the foundations with you, to make sure that you've got the right set-up.

Ensure you understand what you stand for, what you stand against, that you've got the right company, and it is registered accurately. It is also important to have a business plan. Did you know in Japan that they do 25 and 50-year business plans? It is advised to have a really good plan of attack of where you want to be every year. We also do what's called a vivid vision, which is like a three-year vivid vision. So, that we have a good understanding of where we are going to be in three years' time . And then we break that down backwards which then gives us our immediate plans of action. The good thing about a business plan is that it can change at any given time. However, it is really important to have a business plan that you can refer to so you know where you are now, and more importantly, where you're going to be heading in the future, a clear roadmap.

In the beginning we didn't do that, we wanted to do serviced accommodation deal packaging, land development, commercial conversions, raise joint venture finance and, do a couple of lease options. We actually not only confused ourselves but also our audience, because we were trying to do too much too quickly. You will get to a stage where you are building multiple streams of income and perhaps you have a group of companies or your company has multiple services. The thing is you've got to do it at the right time. So, you must position yourself and to do that you need to go deep before going wide. You do not want to spread yourself thin before having a clear idea of the strategy you want to commence with or specialise in. Are you going to start with an investment house? Are you going to focus on raising joint venture finance? Is your main strategy going to be land development or commercial conversions? Or are you going to go out there as a relocation company, and try to work with existing landlords? Therefore, decision making is essential, especially at the start of your process. When you make decisions, you want to be very clear and say what your aim is and how you are going to achieve it. We want you to really start working on your business rather than in your business. A lot of business owners end up spinning all the plates and if you're not careful, you can have a job now instead of a business. A situation where you are working far too hard for not enough money, working hard instead of smart.

As one who will be the decision maker, you want to start practicing being seen and being heard. Commence by never being afraid to tell everyone you meet that you are a professional Property Investor. It may seem small but it is a great place to start. Today social media has made it super easy for us, you can get your message out there to the masses very quickly, easily, and cheaply.

Here is a checklist of things that you need to be aware of

1. What is your company name?

2. Make sure you can go and get the domain name, and we would always recommend you getting (.co.uk and.com.)

3. You are going to want to register your company, typically, it's going to be a limited company.

4. Another step is that you need to start thinking about your branding. This is really important, as it is going to be like your little baby. This is not a hobby; this is a proper business with real people with proper products. So, you've got to set yourself up

Now back when we started out, we positioned ourselves as an investment house. We said, right, we want to be a boutique investment house but we didn't have any money to buy properties. So, we knew that we had to go and raise some money. We asked ourselves; how can we position ourselves as this elegant, five-star sophisticated investment company? We decided to go with black and gold colours for our brand, they were our initials in black, gold and white. And what's happened over the last five years is that we have transformed and evolved. Henceforth, now we go with this nice blue in this nice yellow, and it's a bit more in line with our personalities. Today we are not just an investment house. Now we are a wealth training company. And we've got multiple different products that we offer out to the marketplace. So, what colours resonate with you, your personality and your message?

We have already spoken in previous chapters about vision, values, mission and legacy, so now think about your logo, you're going to want to get your website up and running, bookkeeping, accountants, business cards, brochures, social media platform set up; Facebook, Twitter, Instagram, LinkedIn.

Social media is so powerful, and you are never too old to start. You know, I'm seeing people in the marketplace like Grant Cardone in his 60s, he started on social media only a few years ago, but now he's got millions of followers. You can get your message out there really cheaply and quickly. So, it is important that you are set up onthese social media channels, you're not going to necessarily use them all at once. But what's your preferred channel? Maybe it's Facebook, YouTube, perhaps you're a LinkedIn expert, or you prefer Instagram. You are going to want to start with one or two and then you can repurpose your content and message across multiple platforms.

In our video content we show you how to use social media in your business to get more followers, find deals, find money and ultimately make more money. Have a think about where you want to work, where is your base going to be? We like working from home, but we couldn't work from home full time. We like to have a base and we now have a number of offices for Assets for Life, but when we started, we had no money for an office. So, me and Jay hijacked Portland's Park Hotel, the cost of a cup of coffee or a diet coke a day and we'd pitch up there. Very nice setting. It's not far from where I live, literally five minutes in the car. We used to hold our power team meetings there. When we started to grow a team, we'd have our team members come in there. We ha d our Academy graduates come and meet us when we started to train people. We met investors there; and we had networking events there. It was a great way to start the business. When me and Jay started Assets for Life, we invested 25,000 pounds into training and mentoring. And I (Liam) was able to do that on two interest- only credit cards. And then we found 1500 pounds each, and we loaned that to Assets for Life as our initial startup capital. And now we're turning over millions and millions of pounds. In the training business alone, we turned over more than 3 million pounds last year and, we've also got all our developments. We've been involved with over 18 million pounds worth of property deals; I know what works and what doesn't work. And this is why you are reading this book, because we've got a connection. I want to help you on your journey, but you've got to do the work.

This is why once people do our training, they say, "hey, guys, how can you personally mentor me because I don't know what to do? I need mentoring." There's one thing getting training but there's another thing actually, getting mentoring and hand holding accountability. And that's why me and Jay invest 50-70,000 pounds a year in ongoing training and mentoring Academies. And we would highly recommend our training and mentoring Academy, but have a think, where are you going to work from? Even if it's the local Starbucks or Costa Coffee, and if you are starting this part time, just one or two hours a day, five or six hours a week, you can literally get the power of compound going . The power of compound consistent action on a daily basis will get you the results. Think about bank accounts, payroll, contracts, legal team, processes, procedures and checklists. You want your company to be like McDonald's, you want to be able to roll your business out anywhere in the world at any given time. So, you can start making processes, procedures and checklists. And also, think about a business partner. You don't need a business partner, but if you do decide to have one it always helps to m ake sure your business partner is not your best mate. Best friends are not normally the best business partners. You're better off finding someone that has got exactly the opposite skill sets. Me and Jay are literally like chalk and cheese, he does everything that I am not good at, and I do all the stuff that he doesn't enjoy. You're going to want to build a Power Team, we're going to talk about that shortly. Think about emails, data automation, you can get things like MailChimp and AWeber, where you can automate emails out to your potential investors and business partners. How are you going to take payments ? And again, I'll take you through all of this but equipment stationery is really, really, really important. So, let's now look at St andard Industrial Classification, what we call SIC codes. Every company in the UK has an SIC code and we are now going to talk you through the property SIC codes, so you can decide which one you're going to use when you set up your company on Companies House. 68100 is for the buying and selling of own real estate, 68209 for the lettings and operating of own or leased real estate, 68302 is used for the management of real estate, and 68201 is for renting operations of housing association real estate. Now for pretty much most of you, you're going to use either 68100 or 68209 , or you might end up having a couple of companies doing different things. So, for example, we have a company, which is purely for buying, holding and renting out properties but if we then want to buy and sell properties, we're going to set up another company for this purpose because they are in different tax breaks. And ultimately, when we want to do a rent-to-rent business, we're going to go with 68209 . So, I'm going to talk you through something very important. This is a typical company setup. I want you to be set up legally, to do it in the right way. So, the first thing you're going to want to decide is your company name. And if you're doing rent-to-rent , I would highly recommend that you use the word relocations in your company name, because you're going to set yourself up as a relocations company, where you house different types of workforces across the UK for example, UK workforce relocations. If you are setting up a company, I wouldn't set it out necessarily in your own personal name. So, I wouldn't have Liam Ryan developments because that can prove difficult if I ever want to sell the company in the future. So, have a think about your company name. Then you're going to want to go on to Companies House and register as a limited company, you can either Google company registration and use a company like Companies Made Simple which costs about 60 pounds or you can do it directly on Companies House. Make sure you've got the right SIC code attached, then go and get your bank account set up. You can't get a bank account until you've got your company paperwork.

We use Barclays, I think Barclays are brilliant for property investors. Then you will need your insurances, indemnity and public liability, and a data protection license. You'll need an Ombudsman certainly if you are going to be doing lettings and rent-to-ren t, because you want to be regulated by the same governing body as the letting agents, there are cheaper versions of the Ombudsman, don't use those. You can consider a company like Reeds Rains, it's not a lot of money to register with these guys and when you go into letting agents, you're going to look a lot more professional when you can say, "hey, look, we are the same". So, number seven, association of relocation professionals, ARP is not compulsory. But again, it makes you look good. Certainly, if you're doing rent-to-rent , you will want to make sure you've got your website up and running. If you're doing rent-to-rent , you want to make sure you've got a good understanding of how you work with agents and how you work with corporate clients. I'll give you some examples through the training. And if you're setting yourself up as a property investment company, then you want to make sure your website is very clear that you work with investors, you don't want the website to be over complicated. Literally four or five pages, you want it to be as personal as possible, a few photos of yourself. And ultimately be very clear with your message, you can research other competitors to get a bit of an idea. And of course, look at the Assets for Life website. Don't look at the training part, look at the investment part. And you'll be able to model what we have done at number nine; you'll then make sure you set your email up, and get your domain name. I would recommend that you set up a Liam dot Ryan at info or admin at, get your business cards with your logo. And it's not compulsory, but it can give the feel that you are a much larger company and finally, get yourself an 0800 number. Quite a lot of my graduates that are working full time in their business or their job are getting a lot of inquiries from investors and landlords through their marketing. So, they use an outsourced phone company that picks up the phone during the day. That's something else which you can explore so you can then go to that next level. I hope you found this really useful. But we would encourage you to start now, do the research. Think about your website. Think about your message. Think about your USPS. If you're not 100% sure what strategy you're doing, then, you might not be able to do some of this right now. But at the end of all training, we will come back to the company setup because by then you should be clear on what's going to be your primary property strategy. So, lots for you to be thinking about.

Business Objectives

It's really important you understand where you are now. And more importantly, where you want to go in the future. You've also got to think about what is important for you, your family, and your loved ones. How many deals do you want to do annually? How many hours a week? Do you want to invest? How much money do you want to make? Where do you see yourself in one year, three years, five years? I want you to start thinking about your vision, your legacy, what you stand for and what you stand against.

Now, the question that we will be focusing on is, how are you going to make this happen through properties? James Fox, one of our Academy graduates came into our Academy program which is our mentorship and mastermind program, hand holding process. And he said "Liam, I'm a consultant for O2, I'm not interested in anything else and I'd rather wait a little bit longer and go for the big stuff." I showed him how to do commercial conversions and land development deals and he generated a 2 million pounds profit from his first deals. Now there's a few things for you to think about when choosing your strategy. I want you to think about your personal situation, which of these strategies do you think resonates with you more? When we started this process, I really thought I was going to become a UK nationwide deal packager, you know, a sourcing company, and I invested in some training, I started that process. But after a short period, I realised that I found looking at houses boring, I don't like analysing houses. I'd much prefer to go and raise money. So, not every strategy is going to be suitable for you and your personality and what you want to do. And this is what you need to figure out. Where are your strengths? What are you good at? What can you do more of that's going to bring in more cash flow? Have a think about what you're going to enjoy and think about the area where you wish to invest. And I would recommend an area as we'll discuss later on in the book, no more than 30 to 60 minutes from where you live. Now, there are caveats to this. I personally have a small portfolio and crew in Stoke about three-and-a-half-hour drive away. So that falls out of that particular remit. When I went to do my deals in Stoke, I honestly believed I would be there once a month, I was like, "Hey, no problem." now I can't think of anything worse than d oing that journey once a month, I want to be local to where I am. Now luckily, I've got JV partners there that manage and look after those assets.

And I've actually only been back once since I went the first time in like four years. I've been twice in four years, once to go and have a chat and with my JV partners, I didn't even go up there when I bought the properties, it was over Skype and Zoom. I also know many of my graduates who live in the south, but they invest in the north so, there are exceptions to that. But you need to make sure you understand the upside and the downside which we covered in Chapter three: Site Finding. You also need to think about how much time you can honestly apply to your property business, consider how long you can give of your time weekly, set a target, for example, if you aim to set aside one hour a day, that's 28 hours in a month. Do you know how powerful you can be by investing 28 hours a month? Investing in your education, mentorship, business and growing that compound over months, all of a sudden you would be doing deals, raising money and becoming financially free. We would rather you be consistent daily than do two hours here, 10 hours there then go off the boil for two to three weeks. Consistent action gives you the result. Consistency and repitition. Finally, consider what is important to you, immediate or deferred gratification? Cash flow or big lumps of cash? We see lots of people getting into property who chase the shiny penny, going from one strategy to the other. We'll be honest with you, there will always be bumps in the road no matter what you do in property, you'll be rejected, you'll get the deals that stick, sometimes you'll get the deal and you'll be unable to find the money and other times you'll have the money but you can't get the deal. That's business, that's life. It's about growing and developing; you have to aim to be laser focused. If you are looking for cash flow, to replace your income or to clear your debt then we would encourage you to focus on high cash flowing strategies such as HMOs, serviced accommodation and deal packaging. I love owning assets, but it can take three to six months to buy a property, 18 months to two years to do a land development deal. So, what's important for you now? I'm not looking for an income replacing strategy so I would rather focus on owning assets and this brings me to your 80/20. You have to spend 80% of your spare time on your primary strategy and 20% on your secondary strategy. Do not focus on more than two strategies at the same time. for example, many of our graduates have told me that they only have 10 hours a week to spare and I encourage them to spend eight out of those 10 hours on rent-to-rent, HMOs or serviced accommodation as these are cash flowing strategies. Rent-to-rent deals alone can generate a profit of about 15,000 pounds a year and with two of these deals you've replaced your income and found yourself in a place of financial freedom. So, your 80% might be rent-to-rent a nd your 20% could be land development or commercial conversions which you'll spend the remaining two hours researching, learning and focusing on. Now, this is what I love about property and building a team which provides an avenue to build multiple streams of income. I believe in diversification and having a balanced portfolio. Therefore, once you have your 80% and 20% strategies and you're getting deals, you build your confidence, build a team system with processes and procedures and before you know it your 80% becomes a fully systemised property business. Which consequently enables you to spend more time on your 20% strategy turning that into your 80%. At this point, you can bring in another 20% strategy and you continuously follow this same system until you have multiple property businesses. This is what me and Liam did to build our businesses and now we have multiple income streams. I'm really excited that you are on this journey because if you just follow what I do then you're guaranteed success.

LEGACY

Now, what is legacy? Legacy is what you and your company leave behind, your legacy has to be greater than you.

And let me now share with you what the Assets for Life legacy statement is. At Assets for Life , we want to be remembered for having a positive impact on the world and we want to create 10,000 millionaires or lead people to financial freedom. We are so certain Assets for Life will be carried down to our children and our grandchildren, and I know in my hearts of hearts, that Assets for Life will become an international company, a company that is known for doing good, and for spreading positivity, motivation, inspiration, financial freedom and wealth creation. Assets for Life will still be here in 50 years, 100 years, 200 years. And by having a really strong indication of what you want your legacy to be, this is going to help you stay on track. So, when you're having a bad day or you feel like giving up, when you want to start chasing the shiny Penny or bounce from strategy to strategy, your legacy is going to keep you on track. So, what do you want your legacy to be? How do you want to be remembered? And hey, this is not me being morbid, but if something happened to you right now, what are you really leaving behind? Are you in a position where your family and your friends never have to worry about money again? Are you going to be remembered for doing good in the world? Are you a giver? Or are you a taker? And I truly believe that having a business yes , it's important to make lots of money. But what's really important is to give back to the community. So, I want you to start thinking about what your legacy is.

One part of the Assets for Life legacy that we have not mentioned is our charity projects, we have run a number of projects over the years that we are very proud of. It has always been a passion close to Jay's heart to give back to his r oots in Colombia. for our first project we decided to give to a family in need the chance to build their own home themselves. Jay's former Professor Carlos Ariel Hurtado was already helping poor families in Colombia and we decided to team up with him to help Familia Yande, a family that was living in poor conditions. We raised money through various fundraising challenges in the UK which funded the build of their new house. Andres (dad) told us that his experience building the whole house with his own hands honed skills that allowed him to find a better job as a Construction foreman, thus, transforming his and his family's lives. This was an effect we had not considered and were obviously extremely pleased with. In our view this has been the most rewarding project AFL has undertaken and will continue to be our legacy as a company. In the pictures below you can see some before and after shots with the family:

so much for helping

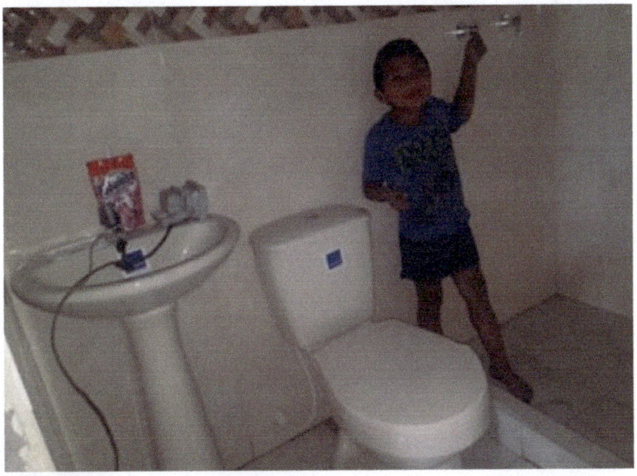

CONCIERTO

Our third project and the biggest to date was to build a nursery for Marta Quilindo an amazing member of the same community as the Narváez family, who looks after a number of children in her neighbourhood for parents who cannot afford childcare. A truly inspiring individual who we are pleased we could help. See below some pictures of the nursery:

In this bonus chapter, we covered the essentials of running a successful property business, emphasizing self-value, core values like trust and quality, and the importance of a strong foundation for long-term success and community impact.

Your business reflects you. The values, dedication, and quality you uphold will define your brand and differentiate you from competitors. Keep these principles in mind as you move forward.

Now, let's put these principles into practice.

Assignment

1. **Identify Your Core Values:**
Reflect on what you stand for and what you stand against. Write down at least five core values that you want your business to embody. These values will serve as the foundation of your business culture and guide your decision-making.

2. **Define Your Mission and Vision:**
Draft a mission statement that captures the purpose of your business and what you aim to achieve. Follow this by articulating your vision for the future of your business. How do you see your business growing in the next five, 10, and 20 years?

3. **Create a Business Plan:**
Develop a comprehensive business plan that includes:
    - Your business name and brand identity
    - Your primary and secondary business strategies (e.g., rent-to-rent, HMOs, land development)
    - Financial projections and funding requirements
    - Marketing and sales strategies
    - An operational plan with processes, procedures, and checklists

4

Set Up Your Business:

- Register your business with the appropriate authorities and ensure all legal and regulatory requirements are met.
- Establish a professional online presence, including a website and social media profiles.
- Set up a reliable accounting and bookkeeping system.

5

Build Your Power Team:

- Identify key roles in your business, such as a partner, accountant, legal advisor, and marketing specialist. Network to find individuals who align with your values and goals.

6

Develop Your Personal Brand:

- Promote yourself as a professional property investor on social media. Share your journey, insights, and successes to engage with your audience and build trust.

7

Plan for Legacy:

- Consider the long-term impact of your business. How will it benefit the community and others? Write down your legacy goals and plan steps to start working towards them.

Completing this assignment is a significant step towards building a values-driven property business. Use the knowledge and tools provided to begin your journey with confidence and determination.

Good luck and may your business endeavours be successful and fulfilling!

CONCLUSION

THEIR STORIES

Hadjer Beyaz

@hadjer.beyaz on Instagram
Date of joining AFL: 2018

My Story

Before beginning my property journey, I was working in Selfridges as a perfume assistant, earning less than £1600 per month. My wages simply weren't enough to cover my bills, rent, and lifestyle. I've always had a deep desire for independence and knew I didn't want to be stuck in a traditional job, but I wasn't sure where to start. I explored a variety of different business ventures, from trading to book writing, but none of them resonated with me. By sheer chance, I found myself in the wrong room at a business event, but I decided to stay and listen. That's when I first heard Liam speak about starting in property, and from that moment, I knew this was the opportunity I had been searching for. I joined the AFL Property Millionaire Bootcamp in late 2018, and that's how I officially got into property. It wasn't easy in the beginning—language barriers, lack of confidence, and navigating a foreign business environment all posed significant challenges. However, a pivotal moment came when my mother was about to be evicted from her home in Algeria. It gave me the drive to push forward and secure my first property. From then on, I never looked back.

Results

Since starting my property journey, I have grown a substantial portfolio that now includes 177 properties across multiple strategies, including Rent-to-Rent, Purchase Lease Options, Serviced Accommodation, HMOs, and single lets. I also completed property flips along the way. Throughout the COVID-19 pandemic, I leveraged opportunities to grow my portfolio from 12 to 45 properties and have continued to scale ever since. I am a multi-award-winning property investor and public speaker, having raised substantial finance for my deals and earning recognition for my success. My business is now thriving, and I'm proud to say that I operate confidently in both property and public speaking arenas.

AFL Experience

Working with Assets for Life has been a life-changing experience. Liam, Jay, and the entire team have provided me with the confidence and strength to overcome the various struggles I encountered along the way. One of the greatest aspects of AFL is that we're learning from people who have already walked the path themselves, and this has been invaluable. The continuous support from the AFL family has allowed me to build my business, gain invaluable knowledge, and continue to learn and grow even as my results improve. I'm still a product of Assets for Life and I'm grateful for the lifetime experience of working alongside such an amazing team.

Rob Mason

Name: Rob Mason
Company: K Suites
https://www.ksuites.co.uk/
Date of joining AFL: December, 2017

My Story

Six years ago, I was stuck in a job that didn't fulfill me, working long hours and feeling like I wasn't moving towards the life I really wanted. I'd always had a passion for business and whilst I'd enjoyed some success previously, I hadn't had the skills or support to take any of my ventures to a scale that changed truly changed my life. When I met Liam and the Assets for Life (AFL) team, I found the key to that took my skills to the next level and beyond and with the AFL family behind me, I finally had the tools and support to build not just one but multiple successful business.

I started my property journey with just one property in Birmingham and I remember how excited I was when that property brought in £2,000 in revenue in a single month. Fast forward to today, I've now managed nearly £10 million in turnover and run not just one but 5 successful businesses. The property management portfolio consists of around 100 properties and covers all corners of the UK. One of my biggest "'why's" from the outset was to have the time freedom and financial freedom to spend time with my kids whenever I want and to travel the world frequently and now, I do exactly that!

Results

In just six years, I've experienced incredible growth, both personally and professionally. Starting with just one property and generating £30,000 in revenue in the first year, my business has now grown to over 100 properties under management, with nearly £10 million in total turnover. My business success has allowed me to create a lifestyle I once only dreamed of—spending more time with my family, taking at least one full day off each week to be with my kids, and travelling the world. Over the course of one year, I went on 20 trips abroad, covering eight countries and four continents. What began as a small management business has now evolved into an ecosystem of multiple ventures, providing several streams of income. I've also been honoured to be inducted into the Assets for Life Hall of Fame after completing over 100 deals, marking a significant milestone in my journey.

AFL Experience

Working with Liam and Jay has been life-changing. They provided me with not only the knowledge and skills to build my property business but also the encouragement and support I needed to overcome obstacles. AFL isn't just a property Academy that teaches you the basics; it's a family that stands by you through every step of your journey. They helped me achieve results I couldn't have imagined—going from £30,000 in my first year to over £1.7 million in just three years.

Liam's mentorship, particularly, helped me realise that I had a mental block when it came to money. With his guidance, I was able to push through that barrier and take action, raising substantial joint venture finance and expanding my business. The AFL family is unparalleled in its dedication and support, and without them, I wouldn't be where I am today.

Tanner Hicks

https://www.tannerhhicks.com/
Date of joining AFL: 2017

My Story

I joined Assets for Life (AFL) back in 2017, during a particularly challenging period where I felt I needed both accountability and support, especially with my mindset. From the outset, Liam and Jay were incredibly supportive and played a key role in helping me get back on track. Very quickly, we realised there was a mutual benefit to working together due to my existing experience in property. My knowledge complemented what AFL was doing, and not long after joining, I became a mentor for the team.

Although I initially joined AFL as a mentee for a short time, I have since progressed to larger deals and have built my own community. My journey has taken me into bigger projects, with multiple commercial conversions under my belt and a current pipeline exceeding £4 million. Through the years, I've raised significant capital from private investors, further fuelling my property ventures. My time with AFL provided me with the belief to achieve more than I could have from the point I met the AFL Team.

Results

Since joining AFL, I've been able to grow both personally and professionally. My mindset has strengthened, I've developed a greater belief in my abilities, and the support I received has been invaluable. I have moved on to do multiple commercial conversions and now have a pipeline worth over £4 million. Raising funds through private investors has been another significant achievement, enabling me to scale my property business. Additionally, I've been able to establish my own community within the property sector, helping others achieve their goals as well.

AFL Experience

Working with Liam, Jay, and the AFL team has been an important step in my property career. What started as a mentee relationship quickly transitioned into a mentoring role, which I've held and enjoyed ever since. It has been so good to see how AFL has grown as a business, community and property family and to be part of that has provided so many positive experiences and memories.

Neil & Jacqui Dobson

Company: The Dobson Property Group
Contact details: ***office@thedobsonpropertygroup.co.uk***
Date of joining AFL: 2019

Our Story

We had just sold our tearoom, which was no longer profitable and needed a new direction and income. Property offered us a steady income and building a pot for the future. It was also a business that we could build together and use other people's money to do.
Challenges- it's all a learning curve, success happens with consistent action, taking one step at a time and believing in the process.

Monthly rental
£9,500

Monthly revenue
£40,000

Deposit
£15,000

Seed Capital
£25,000

1st year T/O
£469,000

AFL Experience

AFL has given us the platform to do things that we didn't even know existed. Being part of AFL gave us access to all the knowledge and the confidence to pursue all our property goals.
They have opened our eyes to all areas of property investment and have helped us to be well rounded property entrepreneurs. There is never an obstacle or barrier that can't be overcome.

Results

We now have over 60 deals under our belt. We have built multiple streams of income all based around property. Liam and Jay invited us to become mentors for AFL in 2020.

We have won multiple awards presented to us by AFL for raising over £1m in JV finance and were awarded mentors of the year in 2021 & 2022.

Our portfolio now stands at £4m and generates £60k per month.

Example Deal

Bridge Apartments – Block of 19 Apartments

Rent to SA

We had an enquiry for rooms for 27 crew members, not ones for saying no, we started to look for multiple houses to rent. Instead, we came across a listing for 1x apartment with 34 rooms!

Within a few weeks we had the keys to a furnished block of apartments, cash flowing from day one as it not only came ready to go but already had guests staying too.

DANIEL STEEL

Company: Relocate Home 4 Home Rentals LTD
Contact details: *@dansteeleofficial on Instagram*
Date of joining AFL: 23/02/2022

My Story

Before diving into the world of property, my life was deeply entrenched in the utility industry. for 14 years, I worked tirelessly on repairing large water mains. I started from the very bottom as a labourer , working hard and learning everything I could about the trade. My dedication paid off as I moved up the ladder to become a team leader, then a supervisor, and eventually, a contract manager. Despite reaching a high position, I found myself overworked and underpaid, which led me to reevaluate my career path.

With my extensive experience and skills, I realised I could step back onto the tools and create a strong team that could be contracted out to larger companies in the water industry. I decided to set up my own limited company, taking on a few teams of well-trained individuals I had mentored over the years. This venture proved to be financially rewarding, and we secured a small but profitable contract. However, the demanding nature of the job took a significant toll on my personal life. I was sacrificing precious time with my family, loved ones, and friends. My own health began to suffer as I struggled to balance work and personal life.

I was caught in the rat race, believing that working harder and earning more was the only way to succeed. But deep down, I knew there had to be a better way. One cold winter evening in October 2021, while browsing Facebook, I came across an ad from Assets for Life, a property and training community. The ad featured a property training program led by Liam Ryan. His message resonated with me, and I felt an immediate connection. It reminded me of my earlier interest in property, a passion I had put on hold due to a lack of knowledge, understanding, and financial means. Taking a leap of faith, I decided to invest £1500 in their three-day millionaire property training program. It was a significant gamble, but I felt the urge to give it a shot. I attended the training in February 2022, and it was a game changing experience for me. The program opened my eyes to new possibilities and provided me with the knowledge and confidence I needed to step into the property industry.

This decision marked the beginning of a new chapter in my life. It wasn't just about financial success, it was about finding a balance and improving my overall well-being. Joining Assets for Life and starting my journey in the property industry has been one of the best decisions I've ever made. It allowed me to break free from the constraints of my previous career and pursue a path that not only provides financial rewards but also brings fulfilment and a better quality of life.

What made you get into property?

The reason I got into property is that it has always been a great passion of mine. I understood that getting into property would allow me to achieve financial freedom and build assets that would grow in value over time. These assets would not only provide me with financial security but also something I could pass on to my future family, ensuring their stability and well-being.

Before attending the Assets for Life boot camp, my knowledge of property strategies was quite limited. I only knew about buying properties at a low value, renovating them, and selling them for a small profit. Unfortunately, I wasn't in a financial position to pursue this strategy at the time.

Everything changed when I attended the three-day boot camp. The program opened my eyes to a variety of property strategies that I had never considered before. The one that really resonated with me was serviced accommodation. I realised that this strategy could provide the cash flow I needed to step away from my day job/Business and focus more time on building a property business. With a small team managing the serviced accommodation, I would gain the flexibility to work on other important aspects of my life.

This was the main reason I chose serviced accommodation and decided to invest heavily in this strategy. Joining the community with Assets for Life was a pivotal decision, not just for my financial growth, but for my overall well-being. It allowed me to make significant changes that benefited my family and health. I learned to value time over money, recognising that financial freedom would give me the time to enjoy life and pursue other passions.

Key challenges along the way

The key challenges I faced began right after leaving the Boot Camp in February 2022. Returning to my day-to-day business, I was contracting myself out as a supervisor on the same contract I had two lads working on. Additionally, I was working for a contractor who was a close friend, and I was essentially his right-hand man, helping run his business with a very small team.

The week I left the Boot Camp, my friend encountered some serious family issues that pulled him away from his business for about six weeks. During this time, I had to step in and manage the operations and financial side of everything. This increased the pressure on me significantly, especially since I had just come off the high of the Boot Camp with so many plans to dive into property training and secure my first serviced accommodation property.

As the weeks went by, I found myself losing the ambition I had felt during the Boot Camp. I had invested around £25,000 in further high-level mentoring and training with the Assets for Life community, and it was disheartening to feel like my investment was being wasted. I also felt unappreciated for the efforts I was putting into my friend's company, which added to my frustration.

Eventually, I decided to step back from my friend's business, which forced the other directors to step in. This allowed me to refocus on my own journey in the property and serviced accommodation industry. It was a tough decision because I didn't want to abandon my friend during a difficult time, but I also couldn't let my own dreams slip away, especially after such a significant financial and emotional investment.

Once I made this decision, my next challenge was balancing my utility business and my role as a supervisor while building a serviced accommodation business on the side. I worked late nights tirelessly to achieve my goals. I spent every free moment speaking to agents, whether during work breaks, lunch hours, or while driving home. I searched the web day and night until I finally secured my first property at the beginning of April 2022.

Outcome

Since leaving the Boot Camp in February 2022, I have built my serviced accommodation business, Relocate Home 4 Home Rentals LTD, from the ground up. I've invested heavily in branding, including a smart car with my company logo and service information.

Today, I have a portfolio of 13 properties. Out of these, 11 are serviced accommodations that I rent out short-term to contractors and working professionals traveling to the Hertfordshire and Bedfordshire areas. Through the Assets for Life community, I met my long-term business partner, and together we set up a separate business. We've acquired an asset on an LPO (Lease Purchase Option) agreement and are currently renting it out under a standard AST contract to a lovely young couple. We invested around £40,000 into this LPO deal, and we're expecting a profit of £40,000-£50,000 within the next year upon sale. This opportunity would never have come my way without the knowledge and strategies I gained from the three-day Boot Camp including meeting my business partner in the community. Additionally, my 13th property is a commercial renovation project. I invested around £12,000 to convert the property into five separate units with shared facilities. These units are now rented out to five small businesses on a rent-to-rent basis, yielding significant profits.

My ambitions continue to grow. Currently, I'm focused on expanding my portfolio, but I have exciting plans on the horizon. In November 2024, I will be starting a new venture in Thailand. I plan to fly out and collaborate with local landowners to develop a platform of luxury, off-the-grid properties, providing unique and exclusive accommodations.

Alongside these international plans, I also aim to create more assets in the UK to ensure future wealth generation for myself and my family. The journey has been challenging, but the rewards and growth have been more than worth it.

Milestones

Throughout my property journey, I've hit several key milestones that I'm extremely proud of. The first major milestone was picking up the keys for my very first serviced accommodation property. This moment was monumental for me, marking the beginning of a new chapter in my life.

Later that year, after securing four more property deals, I was honoured with the Mentee of the Year award at the Assets for Life Christmas Year Awards ceremony. This recognition was due to my hard work, dedication, and commitment to the community. Receiving this award from my mentors was an incredible achievement that not only validated my efforts but also motivated me to continue pushing forward. It inspired me to share my journey, experiences, and knowledge with others, helping them achieve their goals as well.

In March 2023, I attended a business retreat with Assets for Life, where I met two new mentors and experienced significant personal growth. During this retreat, I participated in a program that helped me work on deep-seated confidence issues. By the end of the retreat in Thailand, I felt like a new man. This personal transformation was not only noticed by me but also by my loved ones and peers. Although this milestone wasn't directly related to my property journey, it was a crucial turning point in my life. It allowed me to communicate better, build deeper connections, and gain new business partners for various ventures. This newfound confidence also propelled my success in the serviced accommodation business.

One of my biggest milestones was reaching 10 property deals by late 2023. This achievement was immensely rewarding, as it demonstrated how much I had learned and grown over the past two years. Transitioning into other strategies further validated my progress and opened new opportunities for growth and success.

These milestones, from securing my first property to receiving awards and personal growth experiences, have all been pivotal moments in my journey. They have driven me to strive for excellence, contribute to the community, and continually push the boundaries of what I can achieve in the property industry.

Working with Liam & Jay

From the moment I walked into the Bootcamp, I looked up to Liam and Jay as mentors. Their expertise and stories of coming from humble beginnings to building an empire for themselves and their families resonated deeply with me. They were open and honest about their journeys, and I could see a younger version of myself in their experiences. Watching them present on stage was incredibly inspiring, and it was one of the main reasons I decided to join the

Assets for Life community. The group of successful entrepreneurs within the community felt like a family I wanted to be a part of.

Working with Liam and Jay has been an amazing experience. I've built a strong relationship with both of them, as well as with other mentors in the community. Liam and Jay, as the founders of Assets for Life, have always made it a priority to ensure I have the knowledge and understanding I need. They constantly push me to reach new heights, mentoring and coaching me, and encouraging me to step out of my comfort zone.

I cannot thank them enough for their support and guidance. I've also had the pleasure of spending time with them outside of the UK on several retreats, which has allowed us to build friendships and connect on a personal level. These experiences have strengthened our bond and created a deep connection that I truly value.

Liam and Jay have been pivotal in my journey. Without them, I wouldn't be where I am today. They've helped shape my mindset and given me the confidence to succeed in the property industry. I'm now on the right path, with the right support system behind me. If I ever need help or someone to talk to, I know they are just a phone call away.

Both Liam and Jay are massive inspirations to me, each in their own unique way. I love working with them and being a part of the Assets for Life community. The relationships I've built within this community, thanks to their guidance, are invaluable. I'm excited to see where this journey takes me, knowing I have the best mentors and a supportive community by my side.

Example Deal

SHAUN BARTLE

Company: Blue Wolf Assets Limited
Contact Details: @bluewolfassets on Instagram
Date of joining AFL Inner Circle Academy: March-2021

My Story

Before joining Assets for Life I was working as a qualified accountant, running a tax firm that I helped co-found. We were scaling the business but I was constantly trading time for money, as at this stage I did not have any equity in the business.

I had spent several years before this working in the corporate world in London, before I relocated to the West Country. Unfortunately, like many, I had the wrong information on how to achieve wealth; believing that you had to work your way up the corporate ladder for many years.

I wasn't spending the time I wanted with my family, in particular my young son. I was becoming increasingly stressed with the 9 – 5 and knew that something needed to change.

Property was always part of my goal, but I always believed that you had to have and use your own capital. Joining AFL was the turning point in my journey, as I was able to work closely with Liam and Jay to understand the process of using joint venture finance to complete property deals.

It wasn't always an easy journey. for the first six months I didn't realise that I had a block in my way, which was money. As I had money available, I wasn't pushing myself to raise the joint venture finance; until I had a 1-2-1 coaching session with Liam and we did a deep dive on everything. Once I was consciously aware of the block, I was able to take immediate action by investing my own funds elsewhere and putting myself in a position where I had no choice but to implement the training I had learned.

As with all things in life, the results will only come upon taking action and being disciplined. After several weeks of nothing but massive action, I met with our first potential Funding Partner and followed the diligent process that Liam taught me. We created a win-win situation and agreed the terms for our first £26k of JV finance!

These funds went into our first JV finance flip deal, in which we also used bridging finance and completed our first no money down flip deal. This was a monumental achievement that laid the foundation to go on and complete several more deals, having completed 7 deals at the time of writing.

I have raised over £320k of joint venture finance to date, along with completing 7 deals, which resulted in receiving two prestigious Hall of Fame awards at the AFL Christmas ceremony, which was a fantastic feeling to be recognised by Liam, Jay and my peers.

Working with Liam & Jay

Mentorship is key to accelerating your results and achieving your goals. Working so closely with Liam and Jay and the team at AFL has been truly life-changing.

Due to being a part of a like-minded, successful community, I was also able to invest in a peer and gain access to a rent2rent SA deal, which was not part of my strategy. Collaboration enabled me to receive passive income in an area that I am not an expert in, leaving me to focus on my core strategy.

Not only have I been able to create a successful property business that generates me tens of thousands of pounds a year on very part-time basis, but I have been able to become an elite sales specialist. Coming from an accountancy background, sales is not typically a strong skillset, but the mentoring from Liam resulted in me being able to transition easily.

The knock-on effect of this is that I was able to sack the boss as of December 2023 and go full time into my sales consultancy business and property business. This means I have more time and freedom of choice and I am truly living life on my terms.

My relationships with my family and friends are stronger and we are working towards our family goals on a daily basis. This was only possible with the help from Liam, Jay and the team at AFL.

Having mentors who not only guide and teach, but also hold you accountable is essential for growth.

A mantra that I live by is that collaboration is the new currency and my journey is testament to this.

Example Deal
JV Finance Flip Deal

The strategy on this deal was to flip it. We managed to secure the property BMV, which meant we had a margin on the deal from the outset. The asking price was £80k and we agreed a price of £63k.

This deal was fully financed by £76k of joint venture finance and took 12 months from beginning to end, resulting in a pre-tax profit of over £36k after we repaid the investor. The refurbishment only took four weeks, so this was not only a great profit, but also a fantastic return on time invested.

Ashlee Cave
Company: GCPI and Global City Relocations
Contact Details: @ashlee_cave on Instagram
Date of joining AFL: 20/03/2020

My Story
So, before my property Journey, I was easily working well over 70 hours a week as a secondary school teacher, head of key stage three science and biology. I thought I'd kind of made it, b ut I quickly realised that it really wasn't all it was cracked up to be. I really wasn't enjoying my quality time with my loved ones and friends, because I was always working, even though many believe that if you have all the school holidays you'll be fine but to be totally honest, I was working through most of those holidays. And I actually remember once I had paid for extra carry-on luggage or the extra weights, to

take my laptop and textbooks to Tobago so I can write schemes of work, prepare the lesson resources for the next academic year. So, I was already starting to get myself stuck into learning about ways of increasing or improving my wealth. By trading the forex market as well during that time with some success which I then used to invest into the course with AFL.

I always wanted to get into property so I started watching Homes under the hammer. I knew that many people got their money either from property or then invested their money in property after they made their money through other means. In 2008 when I started University and I saw that there was a major development on what used to be a floodplain in Chelmsford I just figured to myself that whoever is building that is set to make a ridiculous amount of money. I said to myself "Oh I definitely want to be that person one day." So, from that day I turned to my mum and said "I'm gonna get into property, I don't know how but I'm going to do it." That was what set the scenes in me ge tting into property.

A key challenge which I had when starting was the covid crisis. That did definitely take a lot of time out of really getting kickstarted because you know everything was not really moving. So I was learning and applying the skills which I could as soon as everything opened up, with help from Rebecca Ross and other members of the AFL team. I got the ball rolling, and we cracked on with it. I remember we also had one unit which we were set to take on and the landlord just kept moving the key hand over date and the completion of the contracts and eventually he decided to not let the property to us. But the funny thing is, I then got another property and a month later the same landlord actually rang me up and asked me to take the property because the sale fell through. So those were some of the noteworthy challenges I had and I overcame them. And the last one I would say would have been gaining that first investor, The first investor was key. That all stemmed from me posting several pieces of content from when I was absolutely shit to getting slightly better. And he sort of saw that and said "I can see, I've been watching you and let's have a coffee and discuss what you've been doing and perhaps we can do something together". He was my first investor. He began with 5,000 pounds which later became 10, 000 pounds and now he has 30,000 pounds with us as a result of the good return on investment. And he's really happy to work with me for the foreseeable on different property ventures as well as his own portfolio.

I now have a six-figure cash flowing property business, serviced accommodation/R2SA. I am currently looking into applying for some lease options strategies to buy out some of the landlords we work with who no longer want to be landlords, I'm looking to take on multiple deals, blocks and increase my wealth working with many different people. I'm also looking into becoming a speaker and mentoring other new property professionals for the future. Finally, I have turned my day job as a science teacher to my side hustle and now I only teach two days a week by choice to make sure I am giving back and helping those younger individuals, those kids who may not have the best start in life,

Working with Liam & Jay

It has been amazing, the best thing I have done.
I learned about myself, came out of my comfort zone and learned about others in the process.
I became a better version of myself by really applying everything I learned, saw and heard.
My mindset was good to begin with but this really got me thinking more like a V12 rather than an eco-boost engine, I guess.

Outcome

Securing my first award for 5+ property deals
Being a guest on podcasts in North America and Canada
Being a guest on the dealmaker podcast I use to listen to before I started my property Journey
Raising over 60K of finance to date to start and scale the business
Launching my own podcast
Speaking to over 100 people in an in-person event with AFL
Delivering mentor Zooms to Academy members

Example Deal

2 bed 2 bath flat in the heart of Chelmsford with lift access D2V via OpenRent.

Price £1300 pcm agreed for one year initially and now extended to three years at the same price.

This is a R2SA deal which gives me a monthly net profit 1000-1800 on average depending on the time of year after all costs.
Average net profit is approximately £18000 pa

Ola Tijani

Date of joining AFL: 2019

My Story

Before joining Assets for Life (AFL), I was running a petrol station in Essex. Things became extremely tough when the franchise was taken over by a new company that drastically increased the franchise fee, causing my earnings to drop by over 50% overnight. Supporting my family became a real struggle, and I knew I needed to make a change. That's when I came across Liam on Facebook, talking about property. I attended one of the free events thinking I'd learn more about buy, refurbish, refinance strategies. However, after speaking with Liam, he told me that what I needed most at that time was cash flow, and he recommended Serviced Accommodation (SA) as a strategy. I took his advice and went all in.

It took me about six tries to secure my first unit, but once I did, it made me close to £1,500 right from the start. Things only improved from there, and I quickly expanded my portfolio. Today, I manage 14 units, which generate a solid income. I no longer worry about the petrol station or providing for my family. My business is systemised, so I spend very little time running it, and my life has completely changed. I now live on my own terms, take multiple holidays a year, and have even attended AFL's Marbella retreat several times. These days, I mentor others who are just starting their journeys with AFL, helping them to achieve the same success.

Results

Since starting with AFL, I've grown from managing one unit to overseeing 14, generating a steady and reliable income. My Serviced Accommodation business is fully systemised, meaning I spend minimal time managing it. This newfound freedom has allowed me to provide for my family without stress, enjoy multiple holidays each year, and pursue life on my own terms. The success I've experienced has enabled me to step into a mentoring role within AFL, helping others build their own Serviced Accommodation businesses.

AFL Experience

Working with Liam and the AFL team has been life-changing. From the very beginning, Liam's advice to focus on cash flow through

Serviced Accommodation was spot on, and it's what has enabled me to transform my financial situation. The support and training I've received through AFL have been invaluable, and the sense of community within the group is unmatched. I'm grateful for the opportunities and guidance that AFL has provided, and now, as a mentor, I have the chance to give back and help others achieve similar success.

Oliver Roworth

Name: Oliver Roworth
Company: Elisium Developments & Happy Relocations
Contact details: *www.elisiumdevelopments.co.uk, www.happyrelocatins.com, FB, LinkedIn, Instagram*
Date of joining AFL: June 2021

My Story

I was a chartered structural engineer working full time for a salary, had just purchased a house for which I was planning to extend and refurbish as my entry into property, this is when I started searching for training options and came across AFL.

I've worked within the construction and building industry both on site and in a design capacity since my teens and have always enjoyed.

Designing buildings for developers and always aspiring to that role, the potential to make money, property and developments combines my skill set with passion, I love for design, a passion to build and create, feed my ambition, a deep feeling of unfulfillment in my current role especially after achieving chartership, I could see myself in the role, needed a bigger challenge.

Transitioning from full time employment, being out of my comfort zone, learning new skills, the ups and downs of entrepreneurship, the set-backs, running a business, losing SA properties especially at the beginning when first getting started, losing a development deal after investing substantial time money and resources.

I have had 17 rent-to-rent/management serviced accommodation deals for which 6 are still operational, I have secured my first land development deal with a potential GDV of £1.25m.

Working with Liam & Jay

Assets for life has provided me with training to fill the skills gap that I needed to get me to where I wanted to go, which developed my confidence to go after the projects I aspired for, always providing the much-needed injections of motivation after down periods, help keep me on track and provide advice when needed.

Results

Reaching 6-7 operational SA units as this allowed me to transition into developments.

The major milestone for me was securing my first development deal, I transitioned into property to do developments, so employing and training staff to operate the SA business after growing it for 2 years so I could transition into the developments was big, its what I put all the hard work and hours in for.

Example Deal

Land development deal, purchased with planning permission, purchase price £350,000, build cost £575,000, loan interest £100,000, GDV £1.25m, expected profit £225,000, single storey 254m2 house with private access road and two gardens, 4 bedrooms, 4 bathrooms, green roof, air source heat pumps, SIP panel construction, ecofriendly house.

Michele & Elisa

Name: Michele Scafuto & Elisa Bisello
Company: Piazza Lettings
Contact details:
info@piazzalettings.co.uk
www.piazzalettings.co.uk
FB: Piazza Lettings
LI: Piazza Lettings
Date of joining AFL: March 2021

Our Story

Before taking our passion for property seriously, we both had a full-time job and a promising career. We were in what we believed was a good place, something we worked hard for, particularly considering what we had achieved after moving from Italy to the UK a few years back and having the language barrier to overcome, as well as learning a new culture and lifestyle. Then Covid-19 hit. During this time, we found ourselves working longer hours; we were so dedicated to our jobs that most of our time and energy were put into our jobs, to the detriment of our family. We wanted to have our carefree family time back, especially when we found out that our family was growing. It is then that we decided to take our shared passion for property further and make it a business. This was a big step as moving from employee mindset to entrepreneur mindset is a big change. It can be challenging and daunting, and this is where being in a community of likeminded people, mentored by people who have already walked the walk and are there to support you is key. Another challenge we faced was having big "firsts" all at the same time: first time entrepreneurs, first time parents. How we were managing time and energy was extremely important, and efficiency was a must to avoid burnout. This is what lead us to look for ways to systemise and automaise our business, moving from working "in the business" to "on the business" (although we soon realised that parenthood was a totally different story and we needed – and wanted – to be very much involved!).

Today, we look back both with pride for what has been created in three years, for our consistency and tenacity for not giving up when times were tough, and with gratitude for all the people who supported us along the way, and the strong relationships built with our clients and partners. Today, not only do we get to choose our working schedule, but we get to spend all the time we want with our little one. Our business has grown from strength to strength during the past years, and has led us to a new venture: Piazza Lettings, a property management and letting agency to support HMO landlords in the Berkshire and Surrey areas in the UK.

Key Results

Our journey in property has led us to explore different strategies, enriching us with knowledge and experience on a variety of them. Foundational for our journey was our goal of having our family time back, which led us to results very meaningful to us.

We secured our first Serviced Accommodation deal within one month from our training, and we stepped out of the 9-5 and became our own bosses within one year from starting our business.

After joining Assets for Life in 2021, the following year we were given the opportunity to become property mentors in the community. We feel privileged to be able to help and support people who, like us, are on the path towards their freedom.

We were even recognized with awards along the way:
2021 AFL award: Best Female and Male Academy member
2022 AFL award: Most Inspirational

2022 AFL award: 10 Deals achieved
2022-2023-2024 Booking.com: Traveller Review Awards

Assets for Life Experience

Being part of Assets for Life is like being part of a family. It is known that being an entrepreneur can be very challenging at times, with highs and lows. In Assets for Life, the community is there both to celebrate successes and to offer support during tough times, and the sentiment is always collaboration over competition.

Working with Liam and Jay is a treat. Despite their success, they never forget where they started, and this makes them down to earth people. They are not afraid of sharing their challenges; knowing how they overcame them is inspiring and encouraging. Together, they have a baggage of knowledge and experience second to none, and they share it without holding back. They show you the way; help you understand; cheer for you; challenge and push you to become the best version of yourself, as a great mentor would do.

Alan Edwards

Company: Alpus Group
Contact Details: *alan@alpusgroup.com or Alpus Group on Instagram, Facebook and YouTube*
Date of joining AFL: 11 Feb 2023

My Story

I have always worked in property since starting work as an indentured management trainee with a small building company in Portsmouth, Hampshire UK, progressing through larger contractors operating UK wide, then into project management of larger projects of all types including residential, commercial, offices, hotels, infrastructures, heavy and light railways and port works all over the world.

During the 1990`s when I wanted to carry out my own property developments, having already completed several residential refurbishments and conversions, there was a meltdown in the financial market in the UK. T here was a recession and interest rates went up to 15%. I spoke to my Bank Manager about what I had in mind (property development and project management consultancy) and they cautioned me that if I left my job which was as an Associate Director of a successful project management consultancy, they would not loan me any money. As a father with 2 young children and a mortgage I had to do the sensible thing which was to carry on earning a good salary with benefits, rather than take on extraordinary risks with developments, and consultancy.

I am now a full-time property investor and developer who is building an International Group of companies (Alpus Group) centred around property investment and development and education about wealth creation. I have a small and growing portfolio of properties in the UK, Europe and beyond.

Working with Liam & Jay

I have enjoyed working with Liam and Jay and their unique approach to mentorship, it has been a blast ever since the first retreat in Marbella in June 2023, where we did a little open water swimming in rough seas off Marbella through the second retreat in June 2024, and canyon jumping and cliff climbing as team building activities.

I have been thinking bigger following AFL mentorship especially with Jim Francis, and I am currently negotiating a 30m GBP deal using vendor finance, following Jim´s guidance in his book (Eighty Ways To Negotiate a Property Deal).

Outcome

I have project managed many millions of $ value of property and related projects (in excess of $2bn value) over many years starting from the smallest local projects up to becoming Project Director of the highest value ($1.5bn) mixed use developments such as the Crescent Development Project in Baku Azerbaijan , 2010 - 2015.

Essentially what I have been doing throughout my career is managing and protecting "Other People´s Money" on large projects of different types.

Along the way in terms of my own private deals I have carried out numerous refurbishments of houses and flats for investment purposes, including several residential conversions in the UK. I have acquired, held and sold numerous properties in the UK and in Europe. Some of these are now let out as Serviced Accommodation following a high cashflow strategy in the UK.

I am currently following a Commercial Conversions Strategy in the UK although not excluding land development (preferably achieving Planning Gain) or other high cashflow strategies such as Serviced Accommodation and Holiday Lets, acquiring properties using creative finance strategies wherever possible such as Purchase Lease Options, or Vendor Finance.

I have plans to launch an Aparthotel business, being an extension of Serviced Accommodation throughout the UK and Europe.

Example deal

Here is an example of a current deal that I am working on, the numbers are estimates at this time:

4 High Street Alton

Purchase price 400k GBP
15k GBP deposit initially then 385k GBP to complete the purchase upon granting planning permission
Exchange contracts with delayed completion.
Legal costs & Stamp Duty 11k GBP
Design & Construction costs likely 422k GBP
Finance costs 100k
Likely GDV 1.505m GBP (Hamptons)
Profit margin and finance 572k GBP approx. 61%

Less development acquisition and management fees

Andrew Gray

Company: Altitude Property Developments trading under Altitude Enterprises Ltd
Contact details: *Altitude Property Developments on Facebook & Instagram*
Date of joining AFL: 2021

My Story

Before joining I had 1 BTL. I had run my own Audio Visual Business for 12 years, but Covid pushed me to invest in myself and start another income stream. I realised that I cannot rely solely upon my business for income. I reconnected with my dreams of becoming financially free and the goals that I wanted for myself and my family and knew that working with Assets for Life and building a property portfolio was the only way to do this.

I own a small plot of land in North East London that I plan on developing in the future. I knew that I didn't have the skill set, knowledge, experience or contacts to do this and I was impressed with the size of the deals that Liam and Jay were doing. I knew that they could help me achieve this dream.

I knew that I wanted to build a property portfolio, but I didn't know how. I was scared to make the leap as I knew that one wrong deal could set me back financially for years. I was also scared about doing deals that were bigger than your average flip/btl, such as HMO's. I loved the idea of building a HMO but had no idea where to start or the belief that I could do one.

Now I have 2 BTL and 1 7 Bedroom HMO. The properties generate £1500 per month net. I am on my journey of building a property portfolio that will ultimately generate £10,000 per month net.

Working with Liam & Jay

Working with Assets for Life and the mentors has been the catalyst for my property journey. It kicked me into action and gave me the belief that I could do it! Because of them I will be investing in property for the rest of my life and will build a portfolio that I can hand over to my family for generations to come. Being able to have the mentors cross check my deals was invaluable and gave me the confidence to take action. When I hit challenges, the training from AFL reminds me to 'do whatever it takes' to get the project finished and over the line.

Outcome

The main milestone for me was buying a 3 bedroom semi-detached house and transforming it into a high end 7 Bedroom HMO. I have learnt the whole process from start to finish and now I have the confidence to do it again and again.

Example Deal

I bought the property in October 2022 and trusted a property developer, Paul (not his real name), to guide me. He recommended a construction company led by Tony (not his real name) and managed by Tina (not her real name). Tony and Tina had successfully completed large HMO projects before, and Paul assured me they were reliable, with all projects finishing on time, within budget, and to spec. I thought I had everything covered, but I soon discovered otherwise.

In mid-July, I was devastated to learn that the builders had stolen £12,000 in first-fix money and that £4,000 worth of work was needed to correct a poorly constructed dormer. Tony reassured me he would finish the build, even if it meant taking a loss. They considered legal action against the builders, but both Tony and Tina had received threatening messages, and they chose to cut their losses instead. Unfortunately, things got worse when I discovered Tina had been involved with one of the builders. They had stolen the money, shut down the company, and started a new one weeks later. It was a frustrating and costly setback.

By Christmas, the project was far from finished, and I realized my

development finance would expire by the end of March. Tony's team struggled to fix the previous poor workmanship, costing more time and money. By February, with Tony demanding more funds and realizing we didn't have enough to complete the build, I learned Tony had used my project funds to cover his other project, which had also run out of money. I decided to take over, managing all trades and materials myself. Three months later, the HMO was completed, and all rooms were rented within a month, but it came at a significant financial, physical, and emotional cost. Thanks to the support of my family and the skills I gained through AFL training, I now have the knowledge to build more HMOs efficiently. What doesn't kill us makes us stronger.

Purchase Price: £182,000

GDV: £550,000

Loan Repayment to Development finance £330,076

Refinance 75%: £412,500

Money in to Purchase property: £86,850

Additional Costs: TBC

Total Cost: £416,926

Money Added to finish the build: £56,000

Rent Total: £4875 Monthly, £58,500 Annual

Net Cashflow: £825 pcm

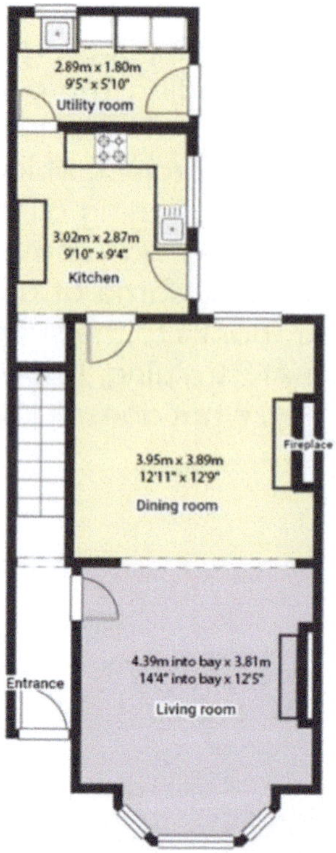
2.89m x 1.80m
9'5" x 5'10"
Utility room
3.02m x 2.87m
9'10" x 9'4"
Kitchen
Fireplace
3.95m x 3.89m
12'11" x 12'9"
Dining room
Entrance
4.39m into bay x 3.81m
14'4" into bay x 12'5"
Living room

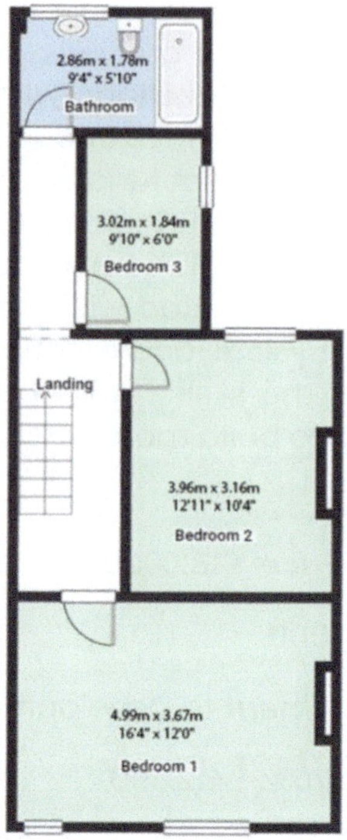
2.86m x 1.78m
9'4" x 5'10"
Bathroom
3.02m x 1.84m
9'10" x 6'0"
Bedroom 3
Landing
3.96m x 3.16m
12'11" x 10'4"
Bedroom 2
4.99m x 3.67m
16'4" x 12'0"
Bedroom 1

FREEDOM
LTD
FOR SALE

FREEDOM HOM

READY TO BEGIN YOUR PROPERTY JOURNEY? SCAN THE QR CODE BELOW TO EXPLORE OUR UPCOMING EVENTS AND FIND THE PERFECT FIT FOR YOU!

ABOUT THE AUTHORS

Liam J Ryan

Liam J Ryan isn't your typical entrepreneur – he's a property wizard, business guru, podcast pro, and best-selling author rolled into one! As the co-founder of Assets for Life, the UK's leading business and wealth training organisation, Liam's all about helping regular folks' level up their lives through real estate. Today, Liam proudly wears multiple hats as a Professional Property Investor, esteemed Property trainer, and sought-after international speaker. So, if you're ready to dive into the world of property and business with someone who's been there, done that, and got the t-shirt, Liam's your guy!

Jay Munoz

Jay Munoz is an obsessed property and business entrepreneur, eco-conscious best-selling author, mentor, and Chartered Civil Engineer with a BSc and MSc. As co-founder of Assets for Life, he helps individuals achieve financial independence through property investment and business education. His written legacy includes "My AFL Journey" and the Amazon best-seller "Property Metamorphosis." Recently, he won a U.K national award for building an eco-friendly passive house and is currently writing a book on affordable green home construction. Jay combines practical strategies with motivational coaching to empower others in property investment and development.